John Craven's Wildlife Report

John Craven

HAMISH HAMILTON
1931–1981

First published in Great Britain 1981 by
Hamish Hamilton Children's Books
Garden House, 57–59 Long Acre, London WC2E 9JZ
Copyright © Introduction, 1981, by John Craven
Copyright © Text, 1981, by Hamish Hamilton Ltd.

Cover photograph reproduced
by courtesy of Chris Fairclough

Designed by Caroline Reeves

British Library Cataloguing in Publication Data
Craven, John
John Craven's wildlife report
1. Wildlife conservation – juvenile literature
I. Title
639'.   QL82
ISBN 0 241 10645 1 Hardback
ISBN 0 241 10701 6 Paperback

Printed in Great Britain by
Morrison & Gibb Ltd, London and Edinburgh

Contents

Introduction

In this world of ours, there are anything up to ten million different kinds of animals, plants and trees. But, by the end of this century, there could be one million less. They will have been killed off – and much of the blame will be ours because we have control over all other forms of life, and often we don't use that power wisely. Some experts reckon that the world is already losing one complete species every day, and soon the rate could be one every hour. It's a grim prospect; let's hope it doesn't happen.

Fortunately, people are becoming more aware of the crisis, and many attempts are being made to protect and save our natural world. There are some who say, 'Why does it matter? People must come first, and we can always see wild animals and plants in zoos or museums.'

But they are wrong. Of course, human beings must have enough room to live, and enough land to grow crops. But we must not be greedy or intolerant towards the rest of nature. Otherwise, in the long run, it will be we who are threatened.

If we chop down trees without planting new ones, the climate will change and deserts will spread. If we don't control our pollution, the soil and the rivers will become poisoned – and it won't be just the fish and the wild creatures that will suffer.

When I was at school, I don't think I ever heard the words 'conservation' or 'environment'. Even if I had heard them, I wouldn't have understood what they meant. Now, they have become part of everyday speech, and the pressure groups that have sprung up to make sure those words are taken seriously have many thousands of members.

I suppose it's television more than anything else that has aroused our interest and concern about wildlife and the threats to nature. Natural history programmes get massive audiences, and the people who present them often become household names.

They bring the concerns of the countryside into our front rooms – although it's not just a one-way traffic. For example, the Young Ornithologists Club has many thousands of members, and lots of them joined after watching television programmes about wild birds. Now, they are out spotting for themselves.

Almost every day there are letters in my mailbag from young people asking for more information about wildlife issues; there are also protest petitions from those who want to stop seal culls or help save endangered creatures, like the whale or the tiger. It's good to see this kind of response, to know that you care. If enough action is taken, perhaps those gloomy forecasts that half the world's endangered species will vanish in the next twenty years will not come true.

In this book, I want you to meet some of the people who have been responsible for creating this awareness, and who have devoted their working lives to preserving different kinds of wildlife. None of them takes a soppy attitude towards the things he or she is trying to protect . . . they are all practical, realistic, and dedicated.

Some of them you will know already from television; David Bellamy, the Botanic Man, and Philip Wayre, a pioneer of wildlife parks who became known as the Otter Man. Philip highlights the fact that it's not just strange animals in remote places that are in danger – the playful, intelligent otter of our own river banks is one of the most endangered of Britain's mammals.

Others in the book will not be as familiar: Peter Robinson is a private detective, but the 'villains' he's after rob nests not people; Kes Hillman describes her life in East Africa among her 'friends', the rhinos; and we go trekking across the Australian outback with Vincent Serventy as he films his country's unique wildlife, and out on to the Canadian ice-floes with Ian Stirling, an expert on polar bears.

Many conservationists work quietly towards their ends, but Allan Thornton is a headline-catcher. He's one of the top men in Greenpeace, the often-controversial group that has become world famous for its campaign to save whales. Among other things, he'll be talking about the moment he thought he might die, when his tiny boat sailed directly between a great whale and the harpoon of a whaling ship!

What binds all these people together is their great love for nature, and especially for those species in danger. And they are all optimists – they all believe it's still not too late to change the way we are spoiling our natural heritage.

As for me, I'm not an expert, just a reporter. I'm a 'townie', born and brought up in city streets, and my love for wildlife and the countryside is one that's shared by millions of others who spend their lives surrounded by bricks and concrete. It doesn't spring from any great knowledge – it's a love from the heart, mixed with a feeling that the countryside and its wild creatures must always be there, must not be put into peril.

I remember once being taken on 'patrol' by a gamekeeper. It had been snowing, and as we trudged along a woodland path, he suddenly stopped and pointed to a spot where the grass still showed through the snow. 'That's where a deer has been lying,' he said. Seconds later, he stopped again. In the silence, the deer broke cover and swam across a nearby stream. He had it in the sights of his gun, but he didn't pull the trigger. The deer scampered across the white hillside on the opposite bank until it disappeared from view.

These few minutes showed me two things. The power that a human being has over the life or death of any other creature, and the certainty that I would have never known about the deer had I been alone. To walk among wildlife with your eyes fully open, you need to be with an expert.

The people in this book are all experts, and I hope that when you have met them you will find that, like me, your eyes have opened up that little bit more.

John Craven
June, 1981

Philip Wayre

Philip Wayre

On a cold, wet day in February, Philip Wayre and I trudged in our wellies across flooded marshland in East Anglia to meet some of his friends, the otters. They were waiting to be fed in their big, open-air pens – and people who think that animals should never be kept in cages, however large those cages are, should ponder on the fact

Two of the Otter Trust's many residents

that there might not have been any otters left in that part of Britain if it hadn't been for Philip.

It was only the second time in my life I'd seen these playful, intelligent creatures with my own eyes, and here in the grounds of the Otter Trust, they were safe. My first sight of an otter, when I was a boy, was not as happy – it was being chased by hounds along a stream in West Yorkshire.

The Otter Trust is Philip's creation and obsession. Visitors can see young otters almost within touching distance: frolicking, making their strange little cries, as inquisitive as the humans who are watching them. In the ponds, the fully-grown otters dodge in and out of the water, amusing themselves as well as the thousands of people who come to wonder at them.

Philip has become known as 'The Otter Man', though he is involved with many other wild creatures as well. He's one of the few people to have successfully bred European otters – which are now on the list of 'vulnerable' animals – and he ranks among the world's leading conservationists.

14

But when he was a young boy, he liked to shoot wildlife, and if he happened to 'wing' a bird, he would try to keep it alive in his parents' garden at Bexhill, in Sussex. The shooting stopped when he was 17, and his interest in birds and animals turned towards protecting them.

He became a farmer, from 1948 to 1958, but he wasn't terribly successful. As he put it, 'I didn't actually go bankrupt, but I got so near to it that two bank officials used to open the door for me when I went to the bank in case I dropped down dead from a heart attack.' After 1958 he gave up farming and started to breed pedigree turkeys and pullets. He also became more actively involved in conservation schemes, joining the Fauna Preservation Society, the International Council for Bird Preservation and the Norfolk Naturalists' Trust. He brought to this work the energy and enthusiasm which highlighted his later, more ambitious projects, and soon he was spotted by Anglia Television, who asked him to introduce a series about animals. This meant filming a huge variety of animals and filling in background information about them all. Each week was different with a new group of animals and a fresh set of discoveries and problems.

As time went on Philip became more and more involved with the animals and the difficulties involved in showing them on film. Very few animals like having a lens pointed at them, and unless cameramen have months to spend on each film, it's hard to capture their real character. Yet Philip wanted to make the rich and fascinating world of animals familiar to everyone, and by doing so to draw attention to the plight so many species were facing. Gradually he began to get an idea of the role he could play.

What he wanted to do first was to set up a place where people, particularly children, could see British and European wildlife in the flesh, rather than on the television or

15

film screen – 'A kind of fairyland where children could wander around and watch many species against a background which was as near natural as we could make it.'

A large number of animals had been acquired in the course of the filming. They would have to be found homes. Meanwhile, here was this large farm on which he was raising turkeys. Why not start putting his ideas into practice? And so, in 1961, the Norfolk Wildlife Park, in Great Witchingham, started. This was the first 'wildlife park' in the UK – in fact it could be said that Philip Wayre actually invented the term.

Making it possible for people to see British and European animals in natural surroundings was just one of his aims. As far as conservation was concerned, something else was very much more important. Too many European animals were disappearing, unable to compete with man. It was becoming vital to try to stop this disaster.

One solution would be to breed European species in captivity. This may sound simple, but it's not. Many European species have become nocturnal: they're very busy at night, and they sleep during the day, so it's very difficult for humans to keep watch on their well-being. Tropical species are often much easier to breed. 'Anyone can breed a lion, given some information,' says Philip.

Nevertheless, Philip was determined to try to stop the decline of endangered European species, and over the years, under his skilful and patient direction, the Norfolk Wildlife Park has achieved a quite staggering list of successes: the first alpine ibex to be bred in captivity in the UK; the first British brown hare; the first green acouci (a type of agouti, a small rodent); the first North American otter; the first European lynx to be bred in captivity for thirty years; the first European wildcat for eighty years; the first Common otter for, remarkably, ninety years . . . and so on. It's hard to point to any one reason why Philip Wayre should have been more success-

16

The first breeding group of alpine ibex in Britain, photographed at Philip Wayre's Norfolk Wildlife Park

ful than anyone before him, but his great attention to detail, sheer persistence and plain curiosity must have played a big part.

Today the Norfolk Wildlife Park has one of the largest collections of British and European mammals and birds in the world. On a trip round the park you can see European bisons, the largest land mammals in Europe; Atlantic and Common seals; all European species of deer; otters; wolverines; wolves; the Brown bear, Europe's largest carnivore; lynxes; Arctic foxes; Golden eagles – and lots more, if you're lucky!

Philip also hoped to bring back animals and birds into areas where once they had flourished. So he bred a pair of badgers – unusual in itself because badgers seldom breed in captivity – and released them on an estate in Norfolk where all the badgers had been killed off. He did the same for European Eagle owls, reintroducing them to the forests of Sweden and Germany.

But by far his greatest triumph in this work has been with pheasants. When he learnt that some types of pheasant were very high on the list of endangered species, and that they would become extinct if somebody didn't do something very soon, he set to work. He began breeding pheasants by the dozen, created the Pheasant Trust to safeguard them all over the word, and was soon sending captive-bred birds back to their native lands, visiting places as far away as Pakistan, Taiwan and the Himalayas. No-one could have done more – or so quickly.

A lot of the animals at the Norfolk Wildlife Park found their way into Philip Wayre's house, either because he took them over when they were too young to live out of doors, or because they were so delightful that they were able to charm themselves into his household, surprising his guests and occasionally terrorizing Gladys, his house-keeper.

Among his animal tenants were badgers, bearcubs, lynxes – and otters. He had always been interested in otters, with their 'quicksilver brains and secretive habits', and in 1964, when he was making a film for Independent Television about the wildlife and natural history of the Norfolk Broads, he was asked to include an otter sequence.

But try as he would, he couldn't get hold of any otters – the European otter was very scarce. However, in those days quarantine regulations weren't as strict as they are now so he imported a North American otter and used her in the film. He called her Limpet. She was only half-tame, but she accepted Philip as a working partner and opened up a whole new world for him. He grew very fond of her and missed her deeply when she chewed her way out of her pen and disappeared, never to be seen again. For a long time afterwards, Philip remembers how 'when I lay in bed on a summer's night, with the moon up and my window open, I fancied I heard her far-off whistle down by the river, and in my mind I saw her flat head rise from the depths of the gravel pit and swim away, the ripples shimmering in the moonlight to mark her going.'

Philip was hooked. Limpet had fired in him a lasting enthusiasm for otters and his ambition now was to breed otters in captivity. To begin with, he managed to get hold of a pair of North American otters, and christened them Rollo and Winkle. They settled in well at the Park and one fine spring day, after keeping everyone in suspense for a long time, Winkle gave birth to three beautiful cubs with dark, velvety grey coats. It was the first time this century otters had been bred in captivity in the UK. As Philip wrote later, 'We, or rather Winkle and Rollo, had done it at last!'

The next step was to try to breed the Common otter, which is found wild in ever-dropping numbers in Britain and Europe, and in slightly different forms right across Asia. This particular type had not been bred since 1881, and it was difficult to find a pair from which to start. Eventually Philip bought a pair of five-month-old Common otters from a pet-shop in London and took them back to Great Witchingham. Gutsy and Ripple, as they were called, took a while to settle down, but they were allowed to run around the house in the evenings and soon got used to human company.

Gutsy was by far the bolder of the two, and his insatiable curiosity and climbing ability created havoc in the living-room. He would turn over the waste-paper basket and rummage through its contents, then pull everything down to the floor for closer examination – vases, bottles, books were scattered everywhere.

He also bit people regularly – not out of malice, but when he didn't get his own way. 'Gutsy's bites eventually became quite a problem', Philip recalls, 'especially with strangers. He seemed to understand that a well-timed nip would allow him to get what he wanted and if a visitor happened to be sitting in a chair he wanted he would jump up and bite without warning!' Ripple and Gutsy also marked out their territory with a characteristic scent – a little like burnt sugar – which tended to cling to clothes. 'Some of our visitors, unaware that we shared our home with otters, often wondered why they smelt odd after sitting in our chairs.'

Eventually Gutsy and Ripple were given an outdoor pen of their own, and about two years later Ripple gave birth to two tiny cubs with short, light grey fur. This was another first for Philip Wayre: the first time this century Common otters had been bred in captivity in the UK.

Other otters followed. First there was Fury, who was found abandoned as a cub on the Isle of Mull off the west coast of Scotland. Her finder hand-reared her, and when she was old enough to travel she was sent to the Norfolk Wildlife Park. Fury arrived 'on a bleak November day,

Ripple and her cubs

bringing her treasured possessions with her, an old piece of sheepskin, a woolly ball and a toy penguin with bells inside it, which tinkled whenever it was moved'. Fury's arrival was a godsend, as Philip explained. 'Here was another potential breeding female to add to our group, who one day would perhaps make a positive contribution to my dream of reintroducing captive-bred otters to suitable wildlife reserves in this country, and so help to ensure the continued survival of the most enchanting of all our wild animals.'

Fury was one of his tamest otters, who always welcomed anyone who went to see her by running to the door and squealing with pleasure. It soon became apparent, too, that she much preferred women to men. She became a 'one-girl' otter and attached herself to Barbara, a member of Philip's staff, allowing her to take liberties – such as taking away her food while she was eating – which no other otter would allow anyone to do.

Kate and Lucy became the next otter members of Philip's household. They were just twenty-eight days old when their mother became too ill to care for them, and Jeanne, Philip's wife, took on the job of hand-rearing them. They had to be fed with Ostermilk from a baby's bottle, and they thrived under the Wayres' care. 'They were the most attractive animals we've ever had,' said Philip. 'Their wide flat noses and tiny blue-grey eyes gave them a permanently doleful expression, and after a good feed, their little tummies distended with milk, they resembled two small brown Buddahs.'

When they became old enough to be housed in a pen of their own, the Wayres continued to keep close contact with them by taking them for long walks every evening. At first they were terrified, staying very close to Jeanne's heels and squealing sharply if it looked as though they were being left behind. But soon they became more adventurous, ranging far afield to investigate the wonderful things that littered the countryside. They also became

Kate and Lucy, aged 14 weeks

more mischievous, refusing to come back when they were called and driving the Wayres to distraction as dusk fell. The otters knew what they were doing, however. They were quite confident that Philip and Jeanne would never abandon them, and as long as they could hear their shouts they felt secure.

Philip was not content with simply rearing otters and breeding them. He wanted to find out all he could about their lives and habits. Soon after Kate and Lucy had been reared, Ripple became pregnant again, and he saw his opportunity to do something that had never been attempted before – to record the otter's complete life-cycle from birth. The BBC jumped at the idea for the *World About Us* television series, and Philip got to work.

The project promised to be difficult right from the start. In the wild, otters give birth in riverside lairs called holts. The cubs are born in complete darkness, and the mother otter is quick to sense any danger threatening her offspring. Although Ripple was quite used to human company and her holt was an artificial one, Philip did not dare to try to film the actual process of birth. Instead he carefully designed a breeding-den and placed cameras and lights in an as secret a position as possible. He transferred Ripple to this den a few weeks before the cubs were due and gradually got her used to the light which would be necessary for filming. He also sat with her for hours every day so that she would become accustomed to his presence near the breeding-den.

Eventually, he was rewarded for his patience and caution. Ripple gave birth, and a few days later Philip switched on the cameras and increased the light. 'For the very first time I peered through the viewfinder to see an otter with her tiny pale-grey, almost white cubs, looking almost as relaxed as they doubtlessly would in a riverside holt. Soothingly I called Ripple's name and she looked up and hugged her cubs more closely. I suddenly realized that she had allowed me into the most secret part of the otter's world.'

He went on to film the day the cubs ate their first fish and the first time they went swimming. He then filmed other otters of different ages, swimming free in the river and behaving just as wild otters would, so giving the film yet another remarkable bonus: wild otters are mainly nocturnal, but here he was able to show in daylight the things that otters normally do only under cover of darkness. Fury, Kate and Lucy were the otters he used in this part of the film, and the Wayres spent many happy days with them as they explored, hunted and adventured.

Only one glaring gap in the record remained – what

actually went on *under* the water? There was really only one way to find out. Philip put on a wetsuit and aqualung, and taking his camera with him, followed the otters on their underwater adventures. The otters didn't mind at all. There were only two real problems: the lack of visibility and an unhelpful cast of actors. All too often the otters were as wilful in the water as they were on land, refusing to do what Philip wanted. But he still got a unique record of the otter in its favourite environment – the water.

I said just now that the otters didn't mind at all. Lucy, in fact, looked on the aqualunged Philip exactly as she would have on land – as her friend, protector and playmate. She often used to sit on his head in the depths, or show him her catch of live eels. Playing with eels was one of her favourite games. Sometimes, they measured nearly a metre in length! Philip, who is not a great fan of eels, found this game less appealing than most.

All the time Philip was swimming in this sea of otters he was still running the Norfolk Wildlife Park, and other animals were demanding his attention. He coped, with the help of his wife, and even found it possible to take animals into their home if they needed special care. Such a one was Grishkin, a European lynx cub which had been born in the Park. Under Jeanne's care, Grishkin changed from 'a round, speckled ball of hissing fury' into a huge, docile 'household cat' with a wicked sense of humour. On one occasion, two bearded men came for lunch. Grishkin had never seen hair on a human face before, and she fixed her eyes on the larger of the two beards. Then she sprang, seized the man around the neck and buried her teeth in his beard, purring loudly. He happened to be holding a glass of sherry at the time and somehow he managed to put the glass down without spilling a drop. Maybe he was used to the extraordinary happenings in the Wayre household!

Gladys, the housekeeper, also suffered from Grishkin's

Grishkin, the European lynx cub with a wicked sense of humour

sense of humour. Philip chuckled as he told me about Grishkin's favourite tricks.

> How Grishkin discovered that Gladys wore bloomers I shall never know, but the result was disastrous. Waiting until Glad was busy cooking with her back turned, Grishkin would choose her moment, then rush in, put her front paws up Glad's skirts, and pull her bloomers down, all in one split-second movement. The first time it happened we laughed so much we couldn't move, in spite of Glad's screams.

All this time, however, otters were the most important creatures in Philip's plans. As he bred and reared them, he thought long and hard about the alarming rate at which the otter populations of Britain and Europe were melting away. It didn't take him long to put together the full, horrifying picture: some species of otter were actually in danger of extinction. I asked Philip why this was.

No-one knows why, exactly, but I think it's fairly well agreed that it started with pollution from agricultural pesticides back in the 1950s. The numbers went down because the otter, like most predators, was at the end of the food chain. The fish and frogs it ate carried a sub-lethal dose of pesticide – not enough to kill the fish or frogs – but when the otter ate a lot of them, they either restricted its breathing, retarded its growth, or bumped it off. So the otter population became very low in the 1950s.

On top of that, there was a tremendous increase in the public use of waterways for fishing, bird-watching, sailing and canoeing. All these things create disturbances which the otter does not like.

What's more, in those days water authorities could be quite ruthless in the destruction of the habitats and wildlife in our wetlands by draining marshes, canalizing rivers, cutting down all the trees and ripping out the vegetation on the banks.

The problem was even worse in other parts of the world. Of the nineteen species at least five were in real danger of extinction, and four of those were in South America, where the fur trade flourishes. Elsewhere, too, the otter was trapped and killed by the tens of thousands, simply to make their skins into clothes.

Philip decided that something had to be done. If otters throughout the world were to survive, they had to get support and protection, and serious efforts would have to be made to study them. And every attempt must be made to put otters, bred in captivity, back into suitable places in the wild. With all this in mind, he and Jeanne, set up the Otter Trust in 1975, with its headquarters at Earsham, near Bungay in Suffolk.

The Otter Trust, set in spare, sternly beautiful country-

A playful otter cub juggling with a rubber ball

side, is a remarkable place. It is bounded by the River Waveney, includes a large lake, a small stream which flows through the enclosures in which the otters live, and 9 hectares of marshland. The Trust and the Norfolk Wildlife Park, are the only places in the world with a proven record of breeding European otters.

Already, the Trust has done great things to safeguard the future of the species. Surveys of otters have been carried out all over the world by Philip and Jeanne Wayre and his scientists and in the UK over 250 otter havens and sanctuaries have been created in cooperation with local landowners. And, of course, otters of all types are reared and bred at Earsham. The Otter Trust is now Philip Wayre's main interest. He still runs the Norfolk Wildlife Park – commuting the fifty kilometres between the two – but it's clear that the otter has pride of place in his heart.

As for Philip himself, he is sixty years old, trim and fit. Apart from being the founder of the Pheasant Trust, the Norfolk Wildlife Park and the Otter Trust, he is a member of the Advisory Panel of the World Wildlife

Fund, and a member of the Survival Service Commission of the International Union for the Conservation of Nature and Natural Resources (IUCN). He has written articles and six books, and has travelled widely.

These days he finds himself increasingly deskbound, dealing with the endless administrative problems of running both the Wildlife Park and the Otter Trust, and this cuts down the time he spends with his animals. He also has to read and write endless reports, and puts together educational packages about animals and conservation for adults and children alike. He feels that people have to be educated about conservation, and he plays his part through his books and the slides he has collected, which are seen by 15,000-20,000 children every year.

'There is a vital need to conserve the environment for future generations,' he says. 'Conservation, after all, is about people – if people don't give a damn about whether animals survive or not, there won't *be* any . . .'

Vincent Serventy

Vincent Serventy with a friendly kookaburra

Australia is a big country. It is the largest island in the
world – a continent all on its own, and a naturalist's
paradise. The climate couldn't be more varied: dense,

29

steamy rain-forests, snowy mountain peaks, arid deserts and endless stretches of pastureland and bush. But, despite the natural richness of this great land, Australia has its conservation problems.

Vincent Serventy has devoted his life to studying and recording the wildlife of his fascinating homeland. A dedicated naturalist, he wrote a book called *A Continent in Danger* as long ago as 1965 sounding the warning that all was not well. Vincent's television programmes, books, films and radio scripts have all helped to spread the message, and now he's more hopeful for the future of Australia's natural heritage; there have been narrow escapes, some battles lost, and some spectacular successes.

'My family has always been interested in natural history,' he told me.

> We lived on a small farm when I was a boy, and had all sorts of pets, like lizards and bandicoots. My brother, Dominic, was the eldest, and used to run competitions for the rest of us. We had to see who could find the first orchid, spot the first nest or hear the first cuckoo of the season. Being the youngest, I missed out on the prizes. But I learned how to look carefully, and the fascination of observing nature closely has never left me.

Vincent went from school to University, and left with a Bachelor of Science degree and a degree in Education. He became a teacher, then a lecturer at a training college. It was there that he began to develop the skills that have made him one of Australia's top wildlife photographers.

> I was put in charge of a section giving advice to teachers about science. I had already started writing and taking still photos, though I wasn't a keen photographer then. But I realised that still photographs couldn't capture the detail of some aspects of wildlife. I wanted to share the

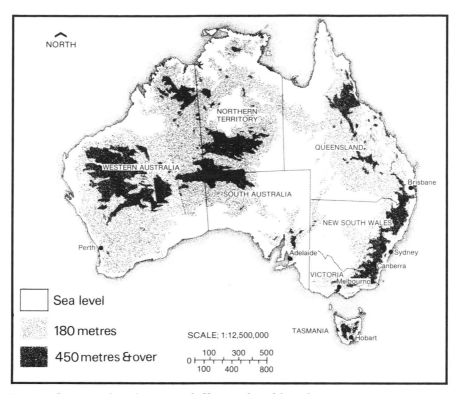

Map of Australia showing different land heights

feeling of excitement I had when I saw animals in the wild. So I turned to the movie camera. In fact, there was one particular incident I'd like to tell you about.

I was sitting in the desert by a waterhole where flocks of budgerigars were coming to drink. I saw a falcon swoop through the green mass of birds, turn, and dive. A wounded budgerigar came skimming towards me, hit the ground behind me and lay, fluttering. The falcon pounced on its prey. I simply couldn't record the episode with my still camera. Such moments in nature are so quick, they can only be captured on film. So I learned how to use a movie camera. It cost a fortune. But I don't regret any of the time or money I spent.

Filming in the snow in Kosciusko National Park, New South Wales

Filming soon became as much a part of my work as writing, and someone suggested that I should do a six-month 'walkabout' and record my adventures for a series of television films.

Now 'walkabout' is the word that Australians use to describe the way the Aborigines (the tribespeople who were there long before the first white settlers arrived) still wander around their vast traditional lands. So I had visions of Vincent, rucksack and billycans on his back, lugging his filming gear across thousands of kilometres of wilderness. Not so! He did make that journey, but in a four-wheel-drive truck, and he took his wife Carol and their children Karen, 8, Cathy, 6, and Matthew who was 18 months. What was it like?

In a word, wonderful! Carol is a keen naturalist, and so are the children. Karen cried when she saw a man knocking down a tree. 'Daddy, he's killed the tree!' she said. Spending six

months with nothing to do but look at plants
and animals was a great opportunity. And we
got paid for it too! The children loved it, and
thanks to really careful preparation, we never
had any serious breakdowns or disasters.

Vincent worked from dawn to dusk on the trip,
shooting all the film himself. He takes his role as a
wildlife cameraman very seriously. 'You have to know
what you are looking at, to understand the creatures and
their habitat. We want to share discoveries with people
who may never see these things for themselves. That's
quite a responsibility, and you have to get it right.'
Vincent spends a lot of time reading other people's
research and even goes to art galleries to study the shape
and form of great paintings – hoping this will help him in
the composition of his own films. The results of this
dedication can be seen in all his work.

On the trip, which he did in 1965, Vincent was able to
get an overall view of Australian wildlife, and to record
some of the little-known, rare and diminishing species of
Australia. But before talking about some of them in
detail, he told me how these unique animals had come to
exist and why, in such vast country, some of them are in
danger.

'To understand all this, I shall have to take you back to
prehistoric times,' he said.

In earliest times, Australia was linked to other
continents by land. But millions of years ago,
this land link was broken and Australia
became the enormous island it still is. For
probably sixty million years, the land was not
inhabited by man. Nature developed in its own
way, without being artificially cultivated. And,
being an island, it was not invaded by animals
from other parts of the world during that time.

Then more than 40,000 years ago, not very
long in the history of a continent, the first men

arrived from Asia. These were the Aborigines, who lived off the land. They used fire sticks as hunting weapons, and later introduced the dingo dog to help them with their hunting. Such creatures as the giant kangaroos and wombats disappeared, as well as other animals and plants that could not cope with fire. Man began to make his impact on the land.

Of course, the Aborigines had been there for centuries when the white man started to come to Australia about 200 years ago with devastating effects. The arrival of deported convicts, gold seekers and later adventurers swelled the population enormously in a very short time. Two hundred years ago, the Aboriginal population was about 300,000. Now, there are more than 13 million people in Australia. But the land hasn't expanded at all, and the same area still has to feed all these extra mouths. Not only that, but Australia exports food too, so land cultivation has been extensive.

The settlers brought sheep, cattle and cats and dogs to serve them in their new land. Today, we need grazing land for 134 million sheep and 27 million cattle. That's an awful lot of land and you can now see sheep and cows across about three-quarters of Australia. Crops cover only about 2% of the land. But the 'new' farm animals, and the wild animals that have always been there, have to share the territory and the food it provides. Pastureland, cultivated to feed the sheep and cattle, now covers large areas of land which for centuries before had been wild bush scrubland. So less and less of the original Australian landscape is left. The old balance of nature is upset.

'And,' says Vincent, 'it's not only the bushland that's been destroyed. So, too, have the forests.'

The pioneers thought every tree was an enemy! They set fire to forest and ringbarked trees. This means that they cut a line around the bark of a tree, which killed it. People wanted to live in the fertile land, to make a better living than they had had in their native lands. They looked upon the forest as a factory area, and tried to get as much from the land as they could. They left a few areas for firewood or timber, and some scrub areas escaped cultivation. But in the places where the pioneers settled, the vegetation of the land changed and this had a profound effect on the wildlife that had always found food and shelter there.

We went on to talk about some of the creatures which have been particularly affected. What was happening, I wanted to know, to Australia's best known animals, the

Kangaroos can jump up to 8 metres at speeds of over 50 kilometres an hour

kangaroo? Like sheep and cattle, kangaroos are herbivores so they have to compete with the farm animals for food and for places to roam. 'First,' said Vincent, 'let me tell you a little about these animals, because kangaroos and wallabies are basically the same. Names vary, but in general, the smaller kangaroos are called wallabies. They range in size from the big grey and red kangaroos, which can measure over 2 metres, to the rat kangaroo, which may be less than 50 centimetres long. As for terrain, some live in trees and some range over open plains and forests.'

Of all the different varieties, Vincent has his own particular favourite – rock wallabies, which can climb up impossible-looking cliffs by means of little 'non-slip' pads on their feet.

There are eleven different kinds, some still common. They may live and breed quite happily in wilder places, but if they know there are hunters around, they hide in the rocks and only come out to feed at night. They often get shot in rocky areas around settlements.

Nail-tail wallabies have a small horny spur at the tips. Like hare wallabies [so called because they hide like hares in long grass and jump very high], the nail-tail is becoming rarer.

Rat kangaroos don't look at all like rats really. They are still quite common in the south-west, but at one time they could be seen all over Australia. These animals have shorter tails and longer snouts than the others and use their tails to carry bundles of grass for nest lining. One, the boodie, digs burrows like a rabbit. [Rabbits and boodies have been known to share warrens.]

Tree kangaroos remind us that a kangaroo ancestor may well have been a tree-dweller, before the tail became modified for hopping on

Tree kangaroos

the ground. These kangaroos have gone back up in the trees to live, and their fore and hind limbs are much the same length.

Kangaroos can destroy crops, and farmers see them as pests. It has been said that a kangaroo eats three times as much as a sheep. And if you consider that the red kangaroo can move at over 50 kilometres an hour, and jump 3 metres high, you can see what a threat they can be to a farmer who wants only livestock on his land. As a result, many kangaroos are shot. They are also shot for meat for export, and for pet food at home in Australia. And some hooligans just shoot them for 'fun'!

There are now colonies of the rarer kangaroos in reserves and parks, though many have forsaken their original territory. We hope some areas may be re-stocked from these reserves, and from surpluses in zoos where they have bred well. But it is worrying to think that if there were a really bad drought, some of our kangaroos could not survive.

From the kangaroo, we moved on to talk about that very strange creature, with a furry body, leathery duck-like bill, tail like a beaver and legs like a reptile – the duck-billed platypus. Said Vincent,

In the bad old days, platypus were hunted for their fur – one coat could take as many as a hundred skins! Today they are totally protected, and are still common from Queensland down the east coast to Tasmania, alongside the rivers, near which they live and where the female lays her eggs. We must keep a watchful eye, though, because the platypus may be in danger from man's use of insecticide. Poison sprays, used to kill insects on crops, get washed into the rivers and so get into the

The duck-billed platypus is now strictly protected in Australia

Koalas live in trees and in the wild are found only in the forests of eastern Australia

systems of the animals living there. As one type of animal feeds on another, the effect of such pollution can be far-reaching. But at least you won't find platypus coats on sale in the shops any more!

Fur coats brought us to the 'real-life teddy bear' – the koala, the wildlife 'model' for the favourite cuddly toy of millions of young children. Had koala skin coats ever been fashionable? 'Most certainly – to the extent that in the early 1900s this animal was slaughtered in its millions,' said Vincent. 'The population decreased enormously. In 1920 it was estimated that as few as 500 were still left in Victoria. This may have been an exaggeration, but the alarm was raised and now the koala is completely protected. Thanks to breeding colonies set up on various islands the numbers are growing so that mainland areas are now being re-stocked.'

You may remember that earlier on in our chat Vincent told me the story of the budgerigar and the falcon. So I checked with him on the situation facing Australia's wild birds. Are any of them heading towards extinction?

I'm pleased to say, not yet. Two sorts of emu have disappeared, and some other species may be on the way out. But attempts are being made to prevent further decline. There are so many birds in Australia which are unique in the world, and which must be preserved from a scientific point of view. But we also get such pleasure from them! We can hear their song, see the beautiful plumage displays, and dis-

A male lyrebird. Its tail feathers were once worn by fashion-conscious women

cover more and more about their strange habits. They must be preserved for future generations to enjoy too.

One magnificent species, the lyrebird, has been saved from extinction. Its wonderful plumage, though rarely seen in full display, was almost its undoing. At one time, the tail feathers of the male bird were very fashionable. In 1896, 500 were sold in Sydney in a few weeks. Five hundred birds had died for a fashion! Laws were introduced, but the slaughter went on. It takes a bird eight years to develop his fine tail and he should be allowed to keep it. Further protection has been introduced, and the fact that lyrebirds can live up to 20 or 25 years helps. They can also run very fast, which is fortunate as they cannot fly away from predators. But there is no longer any fear of extinction, thanks to legislation and changing attitudes.

I'd like also to mention the amazing case of the bird that came back from the dead: the noisy scrub-bird – not a very pleasant name, which some people would like to change to the Australian nightingale, because it sings so beautifully.

It was once common all over the south-west corner of Australia, until the destruction of its home valleys by fire. When none were seen after 1889, it was thought that it had died out because it just couldn't adapt to the way its surroundings were changing. But in 1961, the almost flightless bird was sighted again, by my friend Harley Webster.

We went to see the bird together, and I can't tell you how exciting it was. But we had to stop people from taking 'specimens' and maybe destroying the birds altogether. The authorities quickly put a complete ban on the taking of specimens, not only of the noisy scrub-bird, but of anything else within a 6-kilometre radius of where the birds had been sighted. After a struggle, a site of 5,500 hectares was set aside as a reserve. There is still the danger of bush fire, but a major step has been taken to save this bird from a 'second extinction'.

The budgerigar is not in danger. Budgerigars flock together in tens of thousands

The emu – Australia's national emblem

after nesting, and are difficult to catch on the wing. But they are vulnerable when drinking, as my other story showed.

Australia's best-known bird, as far as the rest of the world is concerned, is the emu – the weird, flightless creature which, among other things, appears on the country's coat of arms. But even a national emblem can damage crops! There was once an Emu War, in 1932, when an invasion of emus threatened the wheat-growing areas and the army had to be called out. Bounty was paid for emus shot, and over 250,000 were killed between 1945 and 1960. In the west, they now use rabbit-proof fences, which don't deter the rabbit much, but do seem to keep the emus out!

We still need to study these birds, so we put 'bands' on them. As they are about 2 metres high, and can weigh 50 kilograms, this can difficult. The birds have to be shot with a drug pellet when they come to water troughs. Once they have been measured and weighed, they are given an antidote to get them back to normal.

Australia is known for its sun and wonderful dry climate, and one of its greatest hazards is the bush fire. Fires can sweep across hundreds of kilometres of bush-land, threatening everything in its path – people, towns and animals.

'There have always been fires in Australia,' said Vincent.

They have prevented the forest over-running some areas and preserved open plains. The Aborigines used fire to clear specific areas. They were skilled fire-raisers, beating it out when it threatened to go beyond where they had planned. For instance, they wanted to preserve the trees that had the right kind of bark for their canoes, or timber for their weapons. Fires also had the effect of burning the tougher plants which might otherwise have stifled weaker ones. Some plants are still only found in areas which have been regularly under fire over the centuries.

I think it was the fire too which almost killed off the noisy scrub-bird. Fire may also have been partly responsible for the thinning out of koalas. Some animals can burrow their way out of danger. But fire is both friend and enemy of wildlife. We need to study its effects in much more detail.

Vincent Serventy with a nesting pair of masked boobies on the Great Barrier Reef

In fact, the need for research, not only into the effects of fire, but also into the way in which different kinds of wildlife live in the same place together, has always been one of Vincent Serventy's great concerns. He's a trustee of the World Wildlife Fund (Australia), and has been busy working on a new television series about endangered animals.

Over the years, Vincent has been involved with many projects, large and small, to save different areas from destruction. Harbour foreshores have been protected, and he battled to save the south-west from hydro-electric schemes and the jarrah forests from bauxite mining. Had television helped him in these battles?

> Most definitely. Television allows people to see for themselves the importance of conservation, even in areas which they are unlikely to visit. We get quite good coverage on television, especially in news programmes. Hopefully, the people watching also get to see that we naturalists are not a load of cranks, but that the questions of the future of our planet affect us all. The Australian public is becoming both more aware of, and more concerned about our national heritage. So much has been lost in the past, due to carelessness, greed and ignorance. We are trying, in Australia, to list all the things in our country that we feel should be preserved. This includes all national parks, nature reserves, areas with special features, historic buildings and so on. We must use the resources of scientific research and information to make sure that the tragic mistakes of the past are not repeated. I think we'll probably win!

After writing at least thirty-six books, and making all those films, I wondered whether Vincent had one outstanding memory – one particular incident – which stood out. 'Well, seeing the noisy scrub-bird after everyone thought it was extinct was a wonderful experience,' he said, 'but I think I'd like to tell you about something that happened in my own back garden.'

Our guests arrived for a party once to find me crouched on the lawn, watching a gaily-coloured wasp digging a hole in it. They got down on their knees and joined me. We decided dinner could wait. Every few seconds the small-waisted wasp would crawl out backwards from her hole, fly helicopter-fashion about a metre from the entrance and drop a mouthful of soil. When the hole was about eight centimetres deep, she stopped working and sunned herself for a while, having first covered the hole with a small piece of bark.

After resting, she hunted around and found a large grey caterpillar, about six times her own size. The fight was on – until she left the caterpillar inert on the ground. She flew a little way away, but returned and straddled the grub. Then she injected it in about a dozen places. It twitched, but it was paralysed.

Again she straddled the caterpillar, then lifted it in her jaws, and headed for the hole. Dumping her burden nearby, she looked around to see that everything was all right, then dragged it out of sight down the hole. In two minutes, she laid her egg on the caterpillar. [The egg would hatch out and feed on the caterpillar.] After the wasp emerged again, she began to pack bits of sticks and stones back into the hole. The top section was filled with sand, pushed in with her legs. Then we saw an amazing thing. Picking up a stone, the wasp hammered away at the soil, firming in the roof. She was actually using a tool, which is rare for any animal! Finally, she scattered bits of twigs to camouflage the entrance.

We had spent half an hour watching this fascinating activity. Many times, I've had to spend much longer waiting to see other wonderful happenings in nature. But it's always been worth it in the end.

David Bellamy

'Conservation isn't putting fences round things and saying, "Ooh, aren't they beautiful"; it's understanding that they are part of the living world on which we all depend', says David Bellamy.

Britain's best-known botanist was at the BBC television studios working on his series *Backyard Safari*, and during a 'break' he talked about his work, his life on and off the screen, and most important, his views on conservation – and let me tell you that he's as friendly and as enthusiastic about his subject in real life as he is on television. With his huge personality and warmth, David has become one of the world's top television 'experts'. On his own he's turned what was the rather specialised science of botany – the study of plants, flowers and trees – into peak-time viewing for millions of people.

But as a boy David Bellamy was not specially interested in botany. He was brought up on the outskirts of London, in Carshalton and Cheam, and although he enjoyed the beautiful Surrey countryside, with its fields and wild flowers, he never felt the urge to find out more about the different species. 'I meet lots and lots of

David Bellamy

children these days who have been turned on by watching television and are very good natural historians at the age of nine or ten', he told me. 'I wish I'd done it that way. As it was, I had to pack an enormous amount of groundwork into just a few years.'

What he remembers most vividly from his childhood years is the Second World War, and the effect it had on people's behaviour. 'It was very exciting – I saw a community of man working together', he says. 'If the girl down the road was getting married, we would all save up our clothing coupons to get her a wedding dress, or we'd collect our butter rations so that she could have a wedding cake.'

When his own home was bombed during the Blitz, the first people to arrive on the scene were the neighbours, bringing food, coffee – whatever the Bellamy family wanted. 'I think it was because I lived through that, that I can understand the living community of the forest, where every plant and animal is working in some way for the good of the community.' These war-time experiences later helped to form what David Bellamy calls his 'very peculiar' idea of evolution: 'I do not believe in the survival of the fittest. Nature never worked like that. It's never been a struggle, it's always been a co-action.'

He firmly believes that everyone has been given talents of some kind, and that we have to find out what they are, and make use of them. His own particular talent only began to emerge when he was already grown up, a late student at university, at the age of twenty-two or twenty-three. 'I was going to be a bio-chemist, and then I met a man called Francis Rose, one of the greatest field-botanists who ever lived. He took me out into the fields and showed me that I could identify the different plants, and remember their Latin names. I suddenly discovered that it was an enormously interesting subject.'

A career in teaching followed. As Dr David Bellamy, he became a senior lecturer at Durham University, passing on his knowledge and enthusiasm to students. That gave him a great sense of satisfaction, he says, and now that he has had to give it up, to concentrate on other aspects of his work such as broadcasting and writing, he misses the university life. 'I personally trained nineteen PhD students, two MScs and hundreds of undergraduates, and they are now out across the world, doing jobs in

Children helping to clear oil from a Cornish beach after the sinking of the oil-tanker Torrey Canyon

practical conservation, teaching at other universities, spreading the gospel to the brighter brains now coming through, who are carrying on the work I've done.'

It was one of his special interests, marine biology, which, almost by accident, brought him into the television limelight in 1967. The oil-tanker *Torrey Canyon* had gone down off the coast of Britain, spilling her cargo into the sea over a wide area, and all of a sudden marine pollution became big news. At that time there had been very little research into the subject, and David Bellamy was one of the few scientists in Europe who was working on it. So he was 'dragged onto television' and interviewed – by me, as it happens – on a beach completely covered in oil. Of that early marine research, he says, 'Very amateurish, I'm sure it was, compared to the work that goes on now, but I think we helped to make people turn round and say, "My goodness, yes, we can pollute the *sea* ..." '

That first television appearance was quickly followed by others. He remembers now, with a chuckle, how he used to watch wildlife programmes by experts such as David Attenborough, Armand and Michaela Denis, and Hans and Lotte Hass, and say to himself, 'One day, when colour television comes along, someone will make programmes like these about botany.' Little did he think that he would be the person to do it! But as his first major series, *Bellamy on Botany*, showed, he, as well as his subject, had a fantastic appeal. People of all ages, many of whom would never think of opening a textbook, found botany fascinating when it was explained the Bellamy way.

After the success of *Bellamy on Botany*, David went on to make programmes all around the world – bringing such varied botanic wonders as the plant life of New Zealand, the peatlands of Poland and the marine vegetation of the Arctic Circle to the television screens of an ever-growing audience. For the series *Up a Gum Tree*, he went to Australia, to show how the unique animal and plant life there has evolved to suit the extreme demands of a very hot and very dry climate. He did his own European tour for *Bellamy's Europe*, taking in the main vegetation zones (by way of Venice and Paris), and adding a light-hearted blend of history and humour to the wealth of scientific knowledge which the programmes put across.

Probably his most ambitious television project so far has been the *Botanic Man* series, in which he went to South America, Africa and Brunei, among other exotic places, to show how plants evolved, and how people depend on them. For the first of these programmes, he went and lived with the Alca tribe in the Amazon rain forest – and this, he says, was one of the most exciting

Members of the Turkana tribe in Kenya, who were filmed for David Bellamy's television programme Botanic Man

experiences of his life.

> These people have an intricate knowledge of the most complicated living-system on earth. They were much better botanists than I could ever be – a child of thirteen led me through the Amazonian jungle, and identified all the plants which were important to them. And they could not only identify them, they could use them in their life, to cure just about any disease they had, or make curare with which to catch the food they eat. I think I learned more from that child than I ever learned from anyone else, and from that tribe, about ecology – because they live as part of the system.

There's no doubt that in the past few years David has done as much as anyone – if not more – to bring to our attention the desperate need to look after and protect the environment. In the university lecture-hall he passed on his knowledge and his message to thousands of students. Now, through the medium of television, he reaches audiences of millions, both in Britain and abroad. 'I think what I try to do is show people the immense interest, and also the immense importance, of plants and animals', is how he puts it, and he is delighted when people come up to him (as they constantly do) and talk with real excitement about botany. 'I get a great cross-section of people writing to me, from taxi-drivers, bus-conductors, and postmen, to very young children of four and five, and at the other end of the scale, white-haired elderly ladies.' A keen diver himself, he also has a great following among the amateur diving world.

There was one remarkable occasion when, while filming in Borneo, he landed by helicopter in the middle of untouched virgin forest, and set off to look at a native dayak longhouse. With great anticipation, he went in – to find the whole tribe gathered round, watching one of his programmes on a colour television set! That incident underlined to him the power of television; it is a responsibility which he takes extremely seriously.

On location for Botanic Man

'What I'm trying to do now', he says, 'is show that we've got to put our conservation house in order.'

> Because if we don't, how can we turn round to a Third World country where people are starving, and say, 'You look after all the furry animals and things so that David Bellamy can show them on his programmes, and David Attenborough can show them on his, and John Craven on his', if we're not looking after our own environment? That is total hypocrisy. It seems totally amazing to me that we can cull one of the rarer large animals in the world – the Faroe Island Grey Seal – to save what, 10p a pound, on 1% of the salmon catch, and then turn round to the Africans, whose children may be starving, and say, 'Do not kill wild animals for food. You must look after your wild life.'

Despite his deep personal involvement with the wildlife of the world, David Bellamy is not sentimental about animals. He believes the needs of humans should come first. When a journalist told him recently that as a child he had been shocked by the conditions of animals in a particular zoo, David pointed out that in those days there were children in Britain living in equally bad conditions – and at least that zoo provided children with an opportunity to see rare animals and learn something about them.

As David puts it,

> In every conservation argument there are always more than two sides. It's no earthly good our saying 'Ah, we must conserve the orang-utang, and the forest it lives in, just because it's a beautiful thing and we like to see it on our television sets.' We've got to remember that we are moderately well-off, and perhaps the people in Borneo, where the orang-utang lives, are not – so they might chop

56

the forest down to sell it for wood to feed their own children. It's a very complicated problem, because if the forest does disappear, they will not have anything at all. There has to be some planning for their future.

What I'm trying to do is to get people in Britain to see that the same is true for them. We are enormously lucky, we live in a pretty pleasant climate, and we've gone through the agricultural revolution and the industrial revolution and still been left with a very beautiful countryside. But the changes which are now going on apace could destroy that completely.

What programmes such as his own are doing, he feels, is spreading the gospel, 'so that more people can see the wonder, and the importace, of a living countryside.'

David Bellamy's television programmes aim to make people more aware of their natural environment

As a champion of conservation in Britain, David Bellamy fought for alterations to the 1981 Wildlife and Countryside Bill, which he and many others felt 'didn't have enough teeth'. He sat in Parliament, listening to the debates and did a lot of 'lobbying' in the hope of getting better protection for those areas of countryside which have special scientific interest. He told me he would have liked to have seen 10,000 children gathered in Parliament Square, looking up at the Houses of Parliament, and saying, 'Now what are you planning for our future?'

Until recently, the British countryside was allowed to evolve in such a way as to become, in David's words, 'a wonderful mixture of natural and semi-natural vegetation, which gives us the way of life – the heritage – which we have'.

> We came through the industrial revolution, which pockmarked the whole of Britain with quarries and so forth – but the interesting thing is that because the pressure wasn't on, and they were left alone, they've all healed up, and so we find peregrine falcons nesting in them. I could show you the most beautiful plant communities in the bottoms of old quarries. But now, because of the enormous pressure of man, we are filling up our quarries with rubbish. We are turning over to massive forms of agriculture – in fact, the heavy industry of the British countryside right now is agriculture and forestry. So we are beginning to destroy this fantastic fabric, this pattern, this heritage.

David Bellamy's books and television programmes have highlighted only too many examples of the harm that man has done, and is doing, to his environment. One typical story was that of the European bison, *Bison Bonasus*, which David showed in *Bellamy's Europe*. A combination of hunting, and the destruction of the deciduous forests where it lived, brought this handsome creature close to extinction – and by 1925 the last wild bisons had been killed. Only the fact that a handful remained in zoos and parks saved the species. A breeding pair was dispatched to Poland in 1929, and today the European bison is doing nicely in its natural habitat.

Another great problem as David Bellamy sees it, is that of inefficient and short-sighted bureaucracy.

> We tell farmers to make their farms more efficient, and they are paid subsidies from the Common Market, and our own government, to do it. But very often they are paid money to produce things that we don't even need – barley, for instance. We don't need all the barley we have at the moment; we're burning it. I'm not saying we shouldn't give farmers the money, far from it; but we should give them the money to protect the British countryside. I guarantee that if you took a national referendum of farmers, and said to them, 'Look, which would you rather have, money from the Government to help you destroy the fabric of the landscape, and make more efficient farming, or money to help you keep the landscape as it is?' they would take the second. Because most of them understand the soil, they like the country – that's why they are farmers! We should put those subsidies into the future – which is the future of our children.

Children play an important part in David Bellamy's life. He lists 'Children' as one of his interests in the celebrities' reference book *Who's Who*, and he and his wife Rosemary now have five sons and daughters, four of whom are adopted. Their son has apparently inherited dad's talent for botany, but David says he'd never push a child in that direction, even though he firmly believes that people can be helped to discover where their talents lie.

There's an enormous sense of seeking inside

David Bellamy and family outside their house near Bishop Auckland, Durham

everyone, and an enormous potential. It all ties up with evolution. If the ancestor of the sea-urchin had found itself in a dried-up creek, it would never have got anywhere, even though it had this enormous potential for living a particular life in a particular environment. As it was, some of them got through, and that is why we have sea-urchins over the whole of the world.

So, if someone *is* keen to discover more about botany, where do they start? Says David,

The main thing to do is to join a local natural history society. Go to your local museum. Join the local country conservation trust, and there you will find yourself working alongside people who are actually doing things for conservation.

The only way to learn – and it's the way I learned – is by rubbing shoulders with the experts. It's much easier, as well as more reliable, than sweating through a book.

He thinks the best 'kit' for studying nature is a pair of binoculars, a handbook for the identification of plants, and, ideally, a microscope. 'With the microscope, you can see the whole of evolution in an ordinary flowerbed.' He's been round the world three times, but says that with the aid of a microscope, every major step in evolution can be seen in your own backyard.

With a good deal of regret, he agrees that today no-one should ever give way to the temptation of picking wild flowers. He says that he did so as a child, and he loved bringing bunches of bluebells and primroses to his mother, but there are more human beings around today, and less wild flowers. It is one of his ambitions, he says, to see a special nature reserve set up where such flowers can be grown plentifully, to be enjoyed and picked by children. Even when beachcombing – one of his favourite pastimes – David Bellamy never takes more than one specimen of any kind of shell that he finds, and he recommends that others do the same.

David has had some fascinating, and rewarding, experiences in the course of travelling the world and making his television programmes. He has dived among man-eating sharks on many occasions, squelched through peatbogs, examined coral atolls, and visited far-flung islands where the birds did not know what human beings were, and acepted him as part of the environment, without any fear. One of the most exciting experiences of all, he says, was living with the Alca tribe in the Amazon rain-forest.

For the future, David Bellamy still has some unfulfilled ambitions. He wants to visit China, Russia and Japan – 'the three big blanks in my knowledge'. He has been trying to get into the Russian peatlands for years. 'I only hope East and West can bury their hatchet', he says.

In Britain he will continue to 'spread the gospel' – writing books, making programmes, campaigning for the preservation of our wildlife heritage, and raising people's awareness of what is at stake. 'If we don't put our conservation house in order, in twenty-five years' time it just won't be worth being a botanist', he told me.

And that, as the millions of people who watch, enjoy, and learn from David Bellamy's programmes know, would be a tragedy.

Kes Hillman

I've always thought there's something rather ridiculous about the rhino. It's got none of the grace and beauty of the lion; none of the gentle strength of the elephant. It's more like a left-over from the age of the dinosaurs.

But despite its unglamorous image, the rhinoceros is a vital link in our wildlife chain and unless something is done soon, that link could be broken and the rhino become as extinct as the dinosaurs.

Leading the campaign to save the rhinos from that fate is Dr Kes Hillman. Not long ago, she took me for a trip in

Kes Hillman

her frail-looking, open-topped car into one of Kenya's game parks to take a look – at rather uncomfortably close quarters – at her beloved rhinos.

She's done a study of twenty-one rhinos that roam the Nairobi national park, doing sketches of each one and giving them 'pet' names, though there's no way that one of these lumbering short-tempered animals could ever become a pet! We set out at dawn, and spotted two or three rhinos during our morning safari.

It was a marvellous, if rather frightening, experience to get so close to these strange and endangered creatures. I asked Kes just how long the rhino had been in danger. 'Not for long, considering the length of time they've been on earth. In the early travel books about Kenya, most of the writers give the impression that the country was crowded with rhino. But in the early 1960s, people like Archie Ritchie, then Chief Game Warden of Kenya, warned they were on the decline. During the last ten years, the danger they are in has become ever more acute.'

The reason for this peril is, of course, the rhino's mighty horn which has always been highly valued as a kind of medicine, and even as a magical potion. Even very small amounts of horn fetch a great deal of money.

It's against the law to kill rhinos in countries such as Kenya, but for poachers the risks are worth it and the slaughter has been terrible. Kes told me: 'We've worked out that there were roughly ten times as many rhinos in Kenya ten years ago as there are today. In ten years' time, there could be none at all.'

Kes had been working in Kenya for eight years now, and most of those years have been spent on projects to do with wildlife conservation. She was born in England but because her father was in the air force she spent much of her childhood travelling and living abroad. But though she lived in many different countries, she never visited Africa. As she grew up, however, she became more and more fascinated by the African people, the countryside and, above all, by the animals. And it was while she was studying zoology in Leicester that she finally decided to try and work in Africa.

So for the next two years she sent off one job application after another – without success. 'In the end', she said, 'I just answered an ad in *The Times* for someone to join a small group travelling through Africa.'

A few weeks later we set off for West Africa where we spent a fascinating six months driving around the countryside, studying and collecting native handcrafts. We also made a few programmes for the local radio station and I took a lot of photographs. Then we drove to Kenya, and by the time we arrived in Nairobi, one of the research grants I had applied for had come through. After that it was simply a matter of getting to know the people who were involved in wildlife and being in the right place at the right time.

Now *she* is on the receiving end of dozens of letters from zoology students wanting to work on wildlife conservation projects!

The first real job Kes had was not with rhinos, but with the African Elephant Group, run by Dr Iain Douglas Hamilton. This organisation had been set up to try and stop elephant poaching. Like rhino horn, the elephant's ivory tusks have always been highly prized by thoughtless humans. But the big upturn in poaching began in the early 1970s when the price of gold went up. Whenever this happens, certain other commodities, such as ivory, also become more valuable. During the 70s thousands of elephants were killed by gangs of poachers, and two-thirds of Kenya's elephant herds were wiped out. Then, the poachers turned their attention to rhinos. Suddenly, rhinos were in just as much danger as elephants.

At the beginning of 1979, a meeting was called in

Elephant tusks for sale in the Sudan

Nairobi to discuss what could be done to protect rhinos in Kenya. Anyone and everyone who was worried about the situation was invited. And, after long discussions, it was agreed they should set up a group to watch over the rhinos. Kes was asked to organise the whole operation.

Today, Kes is chairperson of the International Union for the Conservation of Nature (IUCN) and responsible for co-ordinating efforts to save rhinos all over Africa – not just in Kenya. The IUCN is an international organisation based at Geneva in Switzerland, and its aim is to save any kind of animal or plant threatened with extinction. It works by appointing specialist sub-committees to look into the state of a particular species or group of species. At present there are over a hundred of these spread throughout the world.

'A lot of people think I spend my day in the wildlife game parks fighting off poachers', Kes told me.

In fact, much of my time is spent behind a desk, sifting through letters and reports from all over Africa. When I'm not at my desk, I'm often talking to government officials, trying to get some plan of action off the ground. Not as glamorous as you might think! But, to be fair, there has been a lot ot travelling and I do manage to fit in a fair amount of time in the field – although not as much as I would like.

I asked Kes what the Rhino Group had done first. 'Well obviously the first thing was to find out how many rhinos there actually were. And the only way to do this was to count them. Not an easy job!' I was surprised to find that rhinos, despite their size, are difficult to spot – even from an aeroplane or helicopter.

Unlike elephants, rhinos live almost entirely on their own. You do sometimes see a female rhino with her baby or a couple of adult females together, but this is fairly uncommon. Adult males are even more solitary. Each male has his own territory which he marks out with

A pair of White rhinos dozing in the shade

dung heaps. A Black rhino does this by depositing his dung, scattering it with his hind legs so that they become smeared with it, and then walking around the edge of his territory. If another adult male tries to cross into his territory the first rhino will try to stop the intruder. But he will allow younger adult males to pass through his territory, providing they don't pose any kind of threat.

Despite the difficulties involved in counting rhinos, the Kenya Rhino Group has worked out that there are probably less than 1,500 rhinos in Kenya. But at least the Kenyan government has begun to realise that it must preserve its wildlife if it wants to attract tourists and the money those tourists bring into the country. So Kenya has now got a big loan from the World Bank to set up anti-poaching units, many of them equipped with helicopters, jeeps and guns. These have largely brought poaching in Kenya under control but, as Kes reminded me, the drop-off in poaching could also be due to the fact that it's simply not worthwhile – there are so few rhinos left.

Most African countries have less money to spend on conservation. As a result, the number of rhinos is rapidly dropping and in some countries they are already nearly extinct. In Uganda, for example, it is thought that there are now less than twenty or thirty Black rhinos. In other countries, poaching is taking a heavy toll. Tanzania, for example, has between 3,000 and 8,000 Black rhinos, but those in the north-west of the country are being killed off at an alarming rate. When poaching is brought under control in one country, the hunters move into another where the pickings are easier. So what can the African Rhino Group do – what's their plan of campaign?

We have a 5-point plan – 1. The conservation of habitats; 2. Protection; 3. Stopping the trade; 4. Research; 5. Education. Stopping the trade is the most important priority for the

Black rhinos in Nairobi National Park

long term future of the rhinos, but the most urgent action has to be directed to points 1 and 2. Depending on the kind of rhino, our approach is slightly different. In Africa there are two species of rhino - the Black rhino and the White rhino, though actually they are both dark grey. [The White rhino may have got its name from the Boer word 'weit' meaning 'wide' since it has a very wide mouth.] Black rhinos are smaller than White rhinos and have a pointed upper lip which they use to grasp and tear leaves and branches. White rhinos live on grasses.

There are two types of White rhino, the Northern White rhino and the Southern White rhino. Of the two, the Northern White rhino is in the greatest danger with just a few hundred in southern Sudan and in the Central African Republic (CAR) and only two or three in Uganda. The first priority for them, therefore, is to make sure there are enough conserved

Rhinos are often tranquillised before they are moved to a conserved area

areas for them to live in.

The Southern White rhino also needs more conserved areas, but the problem there is of too many rhinos in small areas. Many years ago, the land where they used to live was taken over for agriculture, leaving less room for all kinds of wildlife. The conservation authorities are trying to set up new parks into which the rhinos can be moved. One of the most recent is Pilansberg Game Reserve in Bophutatswana.

But whatever the species of rhino and wherever they are, they must all be protected. In some countries, such as Tanzania and Zambia, IUCN and the World Wildlife Fund have recently put a lot of money into anti-poaching equipment, and have bought trucks, jeeps, helicopters and guns. In Zambia, the protected areas are patrolled by voluntary rangers under the leadership of a full-time ranger from the government. One of the main areas to benefit has been the Luangwa Valley. Here a 20-man anti-poaching unit has been set up to patrol the whole park both on foot and in jeeps. The Valley has become a wildlife paradise, with vast numbers of elephants and Black rhinos.

But even there, the commercial poaching of elephants and rhinos has rocketed during the last three or four years. Until recently, most poaching was for meat. Now it's almost entirely for horn. I asked Kes how the poachers operated.

Most of them hunt on foot, armed with a variety of firearms, semi-automatic rifles, high-powered sporting rifles and even bows and poisoned arrows. They are constantly on the move, shooting as many bull and cow elephants and rhinos as they can in the shortest possible time. Ivory is cut out on the spot, although if the elephant has been shot with a poisoned arrow, it may take time to die and not be found immediately. Rhino horns are taken as soon as the animal is killed.

Catching poachers in the Luangwa Valley is far from easy because there are large areas of woodland for them to hide in. Also, there are very few roads, and in the early

Poachers cut out rhino horn as soon as the animal is dead

dry season when they are deeply rutted with elephant and hippo footprints, it's almost impossible to use them. In the wet season (November to April) much of the valley turns into a kind of swamp with flooding rivers, tall grass and thick vegetation.

As a result, most anti-poaching operations have to be done on foot. Patrols are made up of several guards with porters who carry food and light equipment for about a week. Patrols keep in touch with each other with walkie-talkies so that they can co-ordinate their movements more efficiently. Hopefully, they will soon have a small plane which they will be able to use for spotting poachers' camps.

But even when poachers are caught, and charged in court, they often receive such light sentences that they soon return to the parks. Many poachers arrested in Zambia have been given fines which are far below the value of the ivory or horn they have taken. And it's not uncommon for poachers to be given back their guns! The result is that they are virtually encouraged to go straight back to the parks and take greater care not to be caught. Sometimes, when that looks like happening, there are pitched battles between the rangers and the poachers. I've been on a patrol with the anti-poaching squad in Kenya and it's just like going to war. The men are camouflaged, well-drilled and armed to the teeth. When they spot a poachers' camp, they crawl through the bush until they are a few metres away, and then go in with rifles blazing.

'Horn must be worth a fantastic amount of money if poachers are prepared to die for it,' I said. 'Yes', Kes agreed,

> although there is very little selling of horn in Kenya now – or at least no legal sale of it. In fact, poachers who have been caught recently have said that there is little point going after rhinos because they can't sell the horn. But two years ago, when horn was selling well, poachers could expect to get about £100 a kilo for it, and that's over a year's wages for many people – assuming, of course, that the poachers could have got jobs. The people who bought the horn could then sell it into the Far East at around £300 to £400 a kilo. There it could be sold for anything up to £600 a kilo – although by this stage the horn would be sold in very much smaller quantities. So you can see that the money was, and still is, big enough for people to take risks.

Kes told me that the vast majority of the horn has been going to the Far East – to China, Japan, South Korea, Taiwan and, more recently, in large quantities to North Yemen. In these countries, every part of the rhino has always been considered valuable – skin, blood and urine as well as the horn. So it's not surprising that the Asian rhino is now virtually extinct. In all, there are now only about 2,000 Indian, Sumatran and Javan rhinos left.

The horn of the African rhino, which is of course the part that is most easily transportable, has been made into precious ornaments, works of art and ceremonial cups. It has also been used to help cure a variety of ailments from typhoid to snake bites, and to help reduce fever.

In North Yemen, rhino horn is used for making traditional daggers called *jambias*. It is every Yemini man's ambition to own a *jambia*, but until recently very few men could afford one. During the 1970s, however, thousands of Yemenis went to Saudi Arabia and the Gulf states to work in the oil fields, where they could earn very high wages. As a result, many more men were able to buy *jambias* and up went the demand for rhino horn.

From 1972 to 1978 approximately 8 tonnes of rhino horn were produced every year to meet the world demand, much of it going to the Yemen. This means that around 2,580 animals were killed every year! Ironically, if you were to ask a Yemeni what his dagger handle is made of, he would probably tell you that it was the horn of a wild animal. He wouldn't know that it was rhino horn.

Clearly then, it's not enough just to create parks and reserves and set up anti-poaching programmes. The only real hope for the survival of the rhino is to ban the trade in its horn. One way this might be done is to persuade the countries that are involved in the horn trade to sign the Convention of International Trade in Endangered Species, of Wild Fauna and Flora (CITES). CITES was started in 1973 with the aim of protecting all species of endangered animals. Once a country has signed, it agrees not to import or export anything to do with any kind of endangered species, and to control the trade in less endangered ones. If a country doesn't keep its promises, other countries can put on moral pressure to bring it back into line. IUCN and CITES countries have recently taken this a step further by requesting *all* countries to stop trading in rhino horn in any way.

Kes out on patrol in Nairobi National Park, Kenya

It seemed to me that it would be a very long time before these measures became law all round the world, and time is something which is not on the rhinos' side. Kes agreed. She also pointed out, rather gloomily, that though there's been a tremendous amount of enthusiasm for the Rhino Group's work over the last eighteen months, this won't go on for ever. There's also a constant shortage of money, and the World Wildlife Fund's money-raising campaign for the rhino is now coming to an end.

How then did she see her own future?

> There are two things I'd like to do. First, I'd like to do some field work of my own instead of analysing everybody else's work; and second, I'd like to write a book about the last eighteen

75

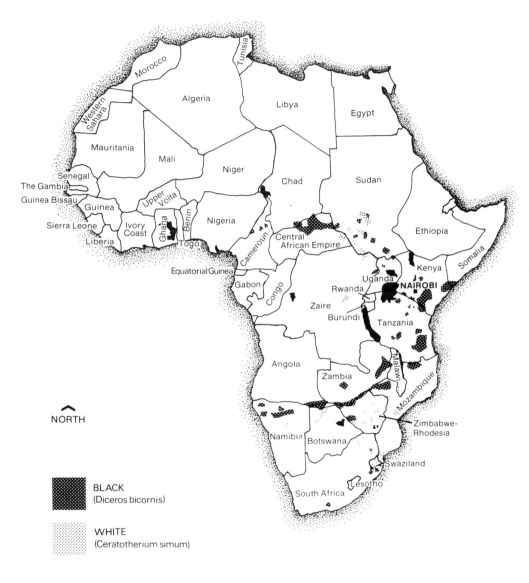

NORTH

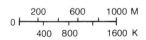
BLACK
(Diceros bicornis)

WHITE
(Ceratotherium simum)

SCALE; 1:40,000,000

```
        200      600     1000 M
  0  ├────┼────┼────┼────┤
        400      800     1600 K
```

Distribution of rhinos in Africa (1980)

months. During this year and a half I've had an amazing time travelling over the whole of Africa and seeing for myself the contrasts between individual countries. People who have never been to Africa often talk about it as though it's one large country, never realising that there are huge differences between, say, Sudan and South Africa.

I asked Kes to tell me about her most interesting experience over the last eighteen months. 'That's such a difficult question', she replied.

There were so many, especially the challenges of flying my aeroplane and driving to the wild empty areas of Sudan. But I suppose one of the most interesting and enjoyable times I had was studying the rhinos in Nairobi Park. Some of these rhinos had been moved there thirteen years ago from areas which were being taken over for agriculture. I wanted to identify each of them in order to look at the long-term success of the operation, and to monitor any future translocations – and that meant getting to know them individually.

I got to know one rhino specially well. He had been caught so that he could be moved to a new park, and he was quite adorable! He was in a pen on his own for about a week and during that time he was given a tremendous amount of attention. One day, when a group of us were standing watching him, he woke up and started to show off. First, he started to squeak which, considering his enormous size, was very funny in itself. Then he sat down on his haunches like a dog and began chewing on a rope that was hanging above his head – and didn't stop until he'd bitten it through. Finally, he went up to the bars and rolled over so that one of the guides could poke a stick through the bars and scratch his tummy. He closed his eyes and sighed with contentment. I think he would have stayed there forever if we'd let him.

'It's times like that,' said Kes, 'that make all the work, the worry and the frustration worthwhile.'

An attention-seeking rhino waiting to be moved to a new park

Peter Robinson

Peter Robinson is a private detective. He's slim, fit, good-looking, decisive – the kind of man who could easily swap places with one of those 'private eyes' on television. But there's one big difference – the villains that Peter is after

Peter Robinson with a poisoned goshawk

don't threaten other people. They threaten the wild birds of Britain.

Peter works for the Species Protection department of the Royal Society for the Protection of Birds (the RSPB), often using the latest scientific techniques to track down criminals who prey on our rarest feathered creatures.

One of his success stories was reported some time ago in the *Daily Telegraph*, under the headline INVISIBLE MARKS GUARD RARE CHICKS FROM THEFT. The report told how the eggs of peregrine falcons had been marked with an invisible code number which could only be seen in certain lighting conditions.

When some of the eggs were stolen, Peter Robinson and a policeman went along to the suspect's house with a search warrant and, having found some eggs, were able to identify them as being those from the falcon's nest. The culprit was caught red-handed. The *Telegraph* added: 'Traffic in fertile eggs and chicks of rare birds, and in particular the peregrine falcon, will now become even more risky following this week's case.' And Peter was quoted as saying: 'This is a victory for both conservation and the law.'

Four illegally taken Golden eagle eggs next to a fifty pence piece

The RSPB is primarily a conservation organization. It has 350,000 to 400,000 members and its headquarters are at Sandy, in Bedfordshire, England. It has 300-odd people working for it, most of them busy on projects like mailing out information and mounting campaigns. The Species Protection department is, among other things, a kind of 'clearing-house' for all information received by the RSPB from the public and the police about possible crimes against wild birds and their nests.

Part of its work is to try to stop crimes being committed. One way this can be done is by mounting round-the-clock watches on nests of wild birds, particularly during the breeding season. Members of the RSPB and local people are always keen to help and, as Peter points out, 'This side of our operation could be compared with the uniformed police force. One of their main duties is to be *seen* and prevent things from happening just by being there.'

The other branch of the Species Protection department is the investigations division, and this is Peter's main preserve. Often it's just not possible to prevent a crime being committed – a nest robbed, or chicks stolen, or an eagle shot – and that's when he and his two colleagues move in. 'In a sense, we are the equivalent of the CID: the plain-clothes detectives. When there *is* a robbery, we work with the police and try to catch whoever was responsible.'

The investigations side of things has been going since 1968. It was set up to help the police enforce the Protection of Birds Acts – the main safeguard that wild birds have in law in the UK – by offering expert advice and generally encouraging them. But, over the years, it has become very much more militant in starting prosecutions and carrying the fight *to* the criminals.

Peter and his colleagues have put a lot of work into this side of things, building up a formidable list of contacts and informants so that now they often know that on a certain day, at a certain time, in a certain place, someone is going to be there with an illegal intent. They can then set up a trap.

In addition, the team makes as much use as possible of modern scientific methods, like that egg-marking technique, and police procedures are closely studied and followed. For, as Peter says, 'I'm a member of the Institute of Professional Investigators, but in many ways I see myself as nothing more than a policeman. That is, it's important that I operate as a policeman would, and abide by the rules which govern police behaviour.'

In the course of a year, Peter and his colleagues in the Species Protection department receive about 1,000 reports of incidents, of which 800 are actual offences. But because of their lack of resources, only a handful can be looked into in any detail. To take on a case involves a great deal of time and money. Some cases are given back to the police to deal with, with the RSPB's help and advice; some are just hopeless. Eventually they are able to reduce the list to about fifty cases which they concentrate on. With such a huge workload the Investigations Section can usually make about thirty prosecutions a year in its own right and be certain of a reasonable amount of success. Generally these will be important conservation cases involving birds like the peregrine falcon or the golden eagle, where it is especially important that the case is handled properly.

As one of three investigations officers, Peter deals with many different crimes. The type of crime that probably takes up most of his time, at least in the early months of summer, is egg-collecting. This doesn't mean that he lies in wait for small boys climbing trees to pinch blackbirds' eggs, and then take them to court. Even though it's illegal to take the eggs of wild birds from nests, the RSPB has a policy of not prosecuting children for this offence. 'When we hear about youngsters doing that kind of thing, we reckon we've come across an interest in birds which is

A Golden eagle with a 3-week old chick

misguided and can be redirected,' says Peter. 'That's what our education department is for.'

What egg-collecting means to him is the raiding of nests by adults, who know that what they are doing is illegal. These people generally concentrate on the eggs of rare birds. Top of their list are eagles, peregrine falcons, and so on – birds with small breeding populations. For example, there are perhaps only 250 pairs of golden eagles in the UK. That's why catching these thieves is so important to Peter and his colleagues.

Early one March one of his informants told him that a known egg-collector would be going to Scotland after eagle eggs during the first week of April. Peter filed the information away in his mind, intending to try to catch the collector in the act of stealing the eggs when the time came. He also managed to find out what type of car the collector had and its registration number. However, on the night of 27th March, Roy Dennis, the RSPB's Highland Officer, telephoned Peter from Scotland. He had learnt that a car and two men had been seen in the

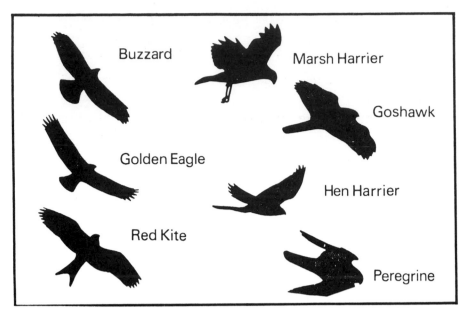

Silhouettes of some of the birds Peter is trying to protect

vicinity of an eagle eyrie in Ardgour. He was convinced they were up to no good, and when he gave Peter the registration number of the car and told him its make there was no longer any doubt.

'In this sort of case you strike while the iron's hot. Scotland's an enormous place, and if you get a lead like that, you don't wait around,' says Peter. The same night he left for Scotland with Graham Elliott, another member of the Investigations Section. They took along a pair of powerful walkie-talkies. They drove all night and rendezvoused at seven o'clock the next morning with Roy Dennis at the ferry, which was the only way out of Ardgour.

Tactics now looked simple enough. Roy told Peter that the collector's car had not left the area all night, so all they had to do was keep an eye on it and find out if the nest had been robbed. If it had, Peter and Graham would stick to the car like leeches while Roy got hold of the police and arranged for the car to be intercepted. They would keep in touch by radio. Alas, the best laid plans . . .

The ferry was half-way across the loch when the car they were after pulled up on the opposite shore, queueing to make the return trip. This was a major problem: the investigators had to be sure that the eagles' nest *had* been robbed, and the police had to be summoned to make the search of the vehicle. But they didn't dare let the car out of their sight or they'd lose it for good. Besides, Peter's face was too well known – if the collector recognised him he'd make a quick getaway. The only thing to do was for Roy to go back on the ferry and tail the collector in his own car, while Peter and Graham followed on the next ferry twenty minutes later, after checking the eyrie. They would keep in touch by radio and as soon as it was practical the police would be called in to intercept the car. But again misfortune struck. Roy lost the collector when the two cars had to go past a road accident, and the collector got away.

That seemed to be that – except that the collector was greedy. Roy and Peter, acting independently but working on the experience of past years, made their way to another eagles' nest they knew about with a history of being robbed. As luck would have it, there was the collector's car. What was more, just a short distance away was *another* car, which was known to belong to another collector.

From now on it was routine. Throughout the day at least one of them kept watch on the two cars. Someone else stayed close to a telephone down in the glen, waiting to hear on the walkie-talkie if the cars began moving. Then he would telephone the police to trigger off the road block. It worked like a charm. Peter was waiting with the police when the two cars came down the road. As soon as the police stopped the cars and the villains recognised Peter, they knew it was all over. Two eggs were found in both cars . . . a fair cop.

There is a sequel to this story. Peter was a little unhappy with the outcome of the case: although the men were convicted and fined, the two from the first car didn't look very bothered. Besides, his spies told him that they seemed to be as active as ever, and that eggs were being exchanged. He put a 'tail' on the older of the two men to find out what he could. A few days later he joined the stake-out and actually *saw* the collector stealing kestrel eggs and taking them home.

That was all Peter needed. He got two search warrants and went to the homes of both men with the police. The result: well over one thousand eggs were found, at least one hundred and fifty of which had been taken *after* the collectors had been caught with the eagle eggs. Prosecution followed: no-one could say they hadn't been warned!

Another type of criminal Peter tracks down are the people who illegally take birds of prey from the wild. These people should be distinguished from those who engage in the sport of falconry – using falcons to hunt for small game such as rabbits – who obtain their birds of prey under licence. But falconry has grown in popularity

A peregrine falcon. There are less than 500 pairs in Britain

over the last ten years and for sound conservation reasons the government issues only a few licences each year. As a result, demand far exceeds supply, and often the would-be falconer tries to buy a bird, such as a peregrine falcon, which the dealer alleges was bred in captivity. In fact, peregrine falcons are very difficult to breed in captivity, and Peter has often been able to prove that the bird actually came from the wild.

A bird bred in captivity must have on its leg a close-fitting ring if it is to be offered for sale. This ring is put on within two or three days of the chick hatching and is fitted so that it cannot be removed from the adult bird's leg. 'This system falls down badly,' Peter said, 'in that anyone with a little bit of cheek and determination can go to a nest with close rings, place them on the chicks and pass them off later as captive-bred birds. Or people can take eggs from the nest and hatch them in incubators, or take a chick from one day old and hand-rear it.'

Peter gave a dramatic example –

> We had one case where a person who was licenced to ring a merlin (a small falcon) with scientific rings issued by the British Trust of Ornithology went to a nest, and when he got there found that the chicks had *already* been ringed. So he called us and asked what was going on. Well, I knew what was going on so we put a watch on the nest. A warden hid in the heather for a week with instructions to keep his eyes open and as soon as something happened to 'phone the police. On a Saturday evening, at about ten o'clock, he saw a man creeping through the bracken with a cardboard box; along came the police and caught him.

Peter Robinson finds one part of his job more distaste-ful than anything else. He had to investigate cases where birds of prey have been destroyed illegally, often very painfully. The people responsible tend to be game-

A merlin hovering above its nest before landing

keepers or farm workers – a tiny proportion from each. 'We're talking about the destruction of peregrines, eagles, buzzards, owls, and a host of other birds of prey – often because the person merely *thinks* that the bird is harmful.'

In the main two methods are used to kill the birds: putting poison baits down, and using hideous instruments called pole traps. Both are serious crimes, although with poison baits it's more difficult to prove the crime. This is because the law allows you to put bait down *under cover* in order to kill rats and mice. All too often, unfortunately, it is laid down in the open, putting wild birds at risk. And excuses like 'I put it down to kill mice' are easy to use as a defence. As for pole-traps, they are still used quite deliberately and more often than you would think. They are gruesome and totally illegal, but few people are prosecuted because, under present law, action can only be taken of there is evidence to show who laid the trap.

Another group of people who occasionally cause Peter trouble are the minority of taxidermists who operate on the fringes of the law, cashing in on the activities of the birds of prey destroyers. (Taxidermists prepare and mount animals' skins to make it look as though the animals are still alive.) 'Once a bird, say an eagle, has been killed, it is passed on to one of these taxidermists, who pays the killer for the carcass. After stuffing it he will get perhaps twenty times that amount from a collector. It's a highly profitable business.'

It's wise not to mention the name of Peter Robinson too loudly if you wander around London's Club Row Market – you might have to leave in a hurry! In the market, and in certain pubs nearby, there's a thriving trade in songbirds, beautiful little creatures that have been trapped illegally and put in cages for sale. The reason Peter's name makes such an impression is because on more than one occasion, thanks to the 'net' of informants he has built up, he has swooped down with a squad of policemen and put dozens of these traders out of business – for a while, at least. But in this, as in so many other crimes associated with birds, the penalties people pay are tiny compared to the damage they do.

Another big business that's against the law but continues to flourish is the import and export of birds which turn out to be rather different from the ones declared on all the proper forms. It's a cunning way of getting round the laws which are supposed to stop rare birds being shipped in and out of Britain. A rare, maybe even endangered, species is listed on the forms as a breed that's more common and unprotected. Peter and his colleagues keep an eye on the market to see what is being sold and work out where it might have come from. So, from time to time, they can provide information which will help lead to a conviction.

The last type of criminal in Peter's casebook is the most hopeless of all: the vandal, who shoots and kills for fun, smashes eggs and tears down nests. 'An awful lot of this sort of thing goes on and these people are almost impossible to track down, unless they're caught in the act. Again, this is where the public can play a part, simply by keeping an eye on the nests.'

Apart from dealing with hundreds of crimes, travelling all over the country, Peter also does a lot of reading. 'I have to study catalogues and magazines for advertisements, just as the police do, and keep myself informed about what is going on and who might be doing it – and how much birds are worth.'

In an average week I'll spend two or three days in the office and two or three days out in the field. Of course, I have to be ready to go haring after a villain at the drop of a hat! Office work is answering letters and queries from all over the world about species protection. And there's the other aspect of court cases – the drudgery: working on the evidence, com-

The RSPB lodge in Sandy, Bedfordshire

municating with solicitors, that sort of thing. At any one time we have at least five court cases going on at the same time.

Out in the field I could be doing anything. It may be a routine case, but there's still a lot of travel involved. We cover the entire UK, so that one day I might go to Doncaster to check an electoral roll to see if someone I suspect of stealing eggs lives there, and I might have a look at his house, or go in with the police and a search-warrant. Then I may have to go to Sheffield in the afternoon to speak to an informant, and on my way back here drive past a couple of houses where I know egg-collectors live and take down a couple of car numbers for future reference. And that won't be a particularly hard day's work. You see, there's so little time and so few of us that I have to try to use the time as well as possible.

Peter feels that there is still a lot that can be done to make their task a little easier, and the future of many rare species of wild birds a little bit more secure. The most pressing need, he feels, is for an official wildlife investigation and enforcement agency to be set up, which would then be equipped with powers the Species Protection department just don't have. At the moment Peter and his colleagues have to rely on the police to make the arrests, and though the police are very cooperative, the liason work takes up a lot of time. Peter points to a sudden increase over the last year in the robbing of falcons' nests. Evidence points to a ring of thieves perhaps with European connections – some falcons are virtually extinct in many parts of Europe – who operate on a scale that the Species Protection department find hard to deal with. A government wildlife protection agency would help enourmously in bringing the thieves to book.

As someone who spends his life trying to make sure the

laws about wildlife are kept, Peter thinks there's a desperate need to make them stronger. Time and again people get away because the wording of the laws is too vague. The new Wildlife and Countryside Bill should help a great deal though.

He would like to see a more effective scheme for the ringing, registration and inspection of rare birds in captivity, and a stricter application of the law on poisoning.

But when all's said and done, Peter Robinson never forgets just how rewarding his job can be. He is doing something positive to help our endangered birds, and every day he's meeting others who are just as concerned, and cracking down on those who aren't. He's learning all the time. 'I never forget that a policeman doesn't simply sit back and wait for the villains to come to him,' he says. 'If we are to make sure that criminals don't destroy our wildlife at will, then *we* must go out and find them.'

Ian Stirling

One of the coldest, bleakest, least welcoming places for any scientist to work is the Arctic Circle, that huge expanse of snow, ice and sea which spreads for hundreds of kilometres around the North Pole. But Ian Stirling has chosen to work there, studying polar bears for the

Ian Stirling observing polar bears at his field camp on Devon Island (north of Baffin Island)

A polar bear's foot. Look how furry and well insulated it is

Canadian Wildlife Service. For three months every year, he sets out into the Arctic wilderness to learn more about these magnificent animals which have no enemy but man.

He's Canadian himself, and his mission is to discover everything about the life of polar bears – their sizes, population, behaviour, and their chances of survival. Not long ago, they were threatened with over-hunting, but now the countries which own the Arctic reaches where they live have signed an agreement to protect them.

It's easy to see why polar bears have nothing to fear from anything but the hunter. The fully-grown male in Canada weighs between 400 and 550 kilogrammes, stands about 1½ metres at the shoulder, and is usually about 3 metres long. The female is smaller, generally between 160 and 270 kilogrammes.

Their fur is, of course, white tinged with yellow, and even the bottoms of their feet have fur in between the thick-skinned black pads. Ringed and Bearded seals are their main diet but in the summer when the ice melts and they are forced on shore, the bears will search around for roots, berries and almost anything else they can find.

But polar bears are much more at home on the ice than on land. They are powerful swimmers, often travelling under water for a minute at a time, and they have been spotted many kilometres from land.

Though Ian has become one of the great experts on these bears, he has always been interested in every kind of wildife.

> I grew up in the mountains of British Columbia and spent most of my free time in the woods, camping, hunting and fishing. This interest led me to read zoology at university, after which I went to work in the Antarctic studying seals

A large male polar bear which has just been 'shot' with an immobilising dart

for a few years. I then returned to do research on polar bears and seals in the Arctic.

During one season, Ian and his team spent 1,714 hours – that's 71 days – watching bears and their behaviour. 'Up there we have daylight for 24 hours,' he told me, 'so we work around the clock in shifts.'

In the spring, when we are doing what we call 'mark and recapture' studies, we set off early, taking lots of food and equipment, and catch bears non-stop until it's dark. In the summer, we often prefer to work at 'night' when the sun is low. The bears are more active then and they stand out better against the snow.

Usually, we 'shoot' them with a drugged dart, and while they are immobile we tag them with a number on their ear. The same number is tattooed on the inside of the animal's upper lip. We also extract a tooth, because this will tell us how old the animal is. In some cases, we may paint them with a special black dye so they can be easily seen from the air in future.

While they are 'knocked-out', they are weighed and measured and we examine them to see what kind of general condition they are in. On later trips, we might recapture the same bears, and then we can tell how far they have moved since they were tagged. In a large sample we can also estimate the size of the population. The bears sleep off the effects of the drug in a few hours.

He told me about an average year in the life of a polar bear. From freeze-up in the autumn to break-up in the early summer, the bears remain on the ice. In some areas of the High Arctic, they can stay on the ice all year round while in other areas, such as Hudson Bay, the ice melts during the summer and the bears must come ashore until freeze-up the following autumn. When the frozen sea breaks up, they move with the ice as it flows, using it for 'cover' while they hunt.

During the thaw, they either go back to the mainland or walk further north, where the sea is still covered with ice. Then, in the autumn when the sea freezes again, they

Examining the teeth of an old polar bear

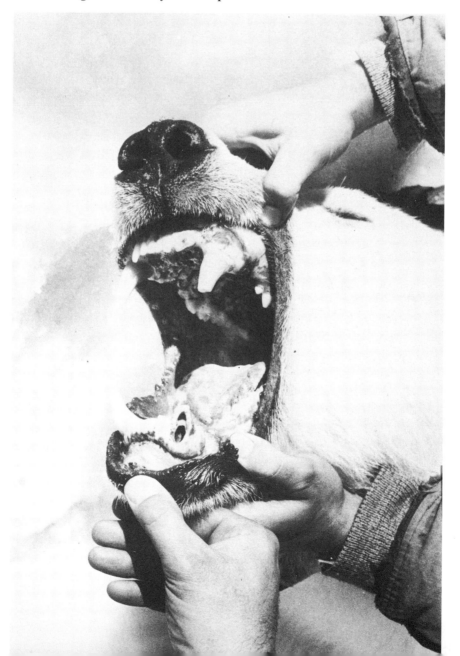

move back on to the ice to hunt. Just how far they move depends on the ice – how thick it is, where it is, and how far the melting ice travels.

If there's a bad storm, bears build themselves dens for shelter. However, it's usually only pregnant females who use a den for any length of time, when they are having their young.

> When she is expecting cubs, which is about once every three or four years, she digs herself a den. Polar bears usually mate in May, but the babies do not begin to grow inside the mother until September. In late October, when the winter is just setting in, she begins to dig.

> First, she makes a narrow entrance which may be several metres long. This passage slopes up to the den itself, which may have one or two chambers with alcoves round the sides and a ventilation hole through the roof. A chamber is about 2 metres long, 1½ metres wide, and 1 metre high. It has to be made where the snow is quite deep, so she chooses a bank of snow, perhaps by a stream or in the lee of a hill-side near the sea. Occasionally, females have been known to dig 'maternity dens' on the drifting pack ice, but as yet we don't know how common this is.

The cubs are born between November and January and at birth they are deaf and blind. There are usually two, weighing about a kilogram each. The mother feeds them on her milk until they reach a weight of 10–12 kgs, when they are big enough to go outside the den for short periods.

During this time, the mother lives off her own fat, so when she comes out of the den she is very much thinner than when she went in. The family doesn't go far away from the den at this stage, and the entrance is surrounded with the tracks of the young cubs where they've been digging or sliding down snow-banks!

Later, the family leaves the den and heads towards the sea to begin hunting. The cubs stay with the mother for about two and a half years.

A female polar bear and her two 2½ year old cubs walking on the ice

During that time, they learn to hunt and kill the Ringed and Bearded seals that are their main source of food. Their favourite tactic is what's known as 'still' hunting. The bear stands, sits or lies – quite still – beside a 'breathing hole' which a seal has made in the ice so that it can come up for air. The seals stop these holes freezing over by scraping at the ice as it forms; they have heavy claws on their fore-flippers to help them.

In some places, the ice keeps on cracking because of

A young Ringed seal – the main food of the polar bear

winds, tides or currents, and these are the best hunting places for bears – if the hole is open, the bear just has to wait for a seal to break the surface, and then pounce. If the hole is covered by snow, the bear has to dig its way through.

Usually, bears track down these breathing holes by using their sense of smell. Says Ian,

> The bears must make sure they pounce right on their target, otherwise the seals have a chance of getting away. It probably takes a long time to develop this skill.

> We have often watched bears when they have found a seal's 'lair' under the ice. They pause for a time, quite still, and wait. Then they suddenly rush forward and smash straight through the ice with their powerful fore-legs.

When we've checked later, we've found that the bears have always jumped in right over the breathing hole!

The young bears learn to hunt by watching their mother. They watch what she does, and imitate her. Two-year-old cubs still follow their mother, but not so closely. They might be a few kilometres away from her while she's hunting.

In the spring, cubs do hardly any hunting at all. This is because the breathing holes are covered by hard snow, and the little ones aren't heavy enough to break through quickly enough. The snow can be anything from 30 to 70 centimetres thick.

As you'll have gathered, Ian spends a great deal of time studying polar bears. Most of the tagging work is done between late March and early May when the animals are on the snow-covered ice-floes near the coast. His team can spot their tracks in the snow, and that makes it easier to find the bears.

'At this time too, mother bears are coming out of the dens with their cubs,' explained Ian, 'and males are looking for females to mate with. And, fortunately for us,

A half-drugged bear before it is 'tagged'

the weather is quite settled. In the summer we can't see their tracks on the land or on the bare ice, and bears are very fat then so it's more difficult to drug them.'

The team has to be very careful not to disturb mother bears in their dens, otherwise they'll probably abandon their cubs and may never make another den in the same area. And the cubs stand no chance of survival if their mother leaves them.

For Ian, then, springtime in the Arctic is a hectic time, working round the clock tagging, checking, making notes, and watching the movements of bears through telescopes.

Much of the rest of the year is spent in his laboratory in Edmonton, Alberta, analysing all the information gathered out in the icefields, writing reports and planning new projects. There's also a lot of office work. 'I find that I'm barraged with telephone calls and letters to be answered,' he said. 'People from all over the world want information about polar bears. They want to know about their biology

Ian's pilot, Gene Burleson, holds a polar bear cub while its mother is drugged

Come in Number 96! A polar bear which has been painted with a special black dye so that it can be recognised from the air

– and how to avoid being eaten by them! And my laboratory also provides training and advice for other people who are working either with polar bears or in the Arctic.'

Until Ian told me about the way polar bears catch seals, I had never realised just how skilled polar bears are at hunting. But these great hunters are themselves in danger – from human killers. Fortunately, there are now strict laws to protect them; in 1973 Canada, Norway, Denmark, the United States and the Soviet Union – the countries in whose Arctic territories the bears live – signed an agreement to conserve them. This kind of international co-operation is vital because the bears wander at will, not knowing about the borders which we humans set up. Before the agreement it wasn't easy to discover what each country was doing in the way of research and conservation. Now, with wider knowledge, scientists can recommend how the bears should be

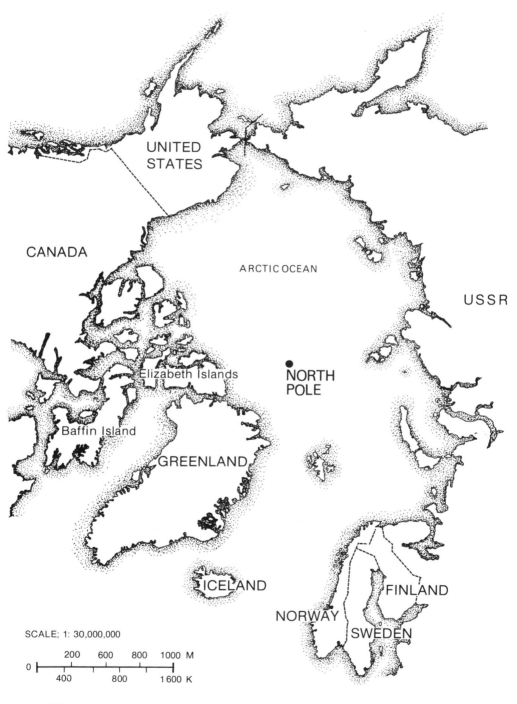

UNITED
STATES

CANADA

ARCTIC OCEAN

USSR

Elizabeth Islands

NORTH
POLE

Baffin Island

GREENLAND

ICELAND

FINLAND

NORWAY

SWEDEN

SCALE; 1: 30,000,000

```
        200    600    800   1000 M
0
        400          800          1600 K
```

The Arctic

'managed' and make forecasts about when and how they are likely to be at risk.

It's research by people like Ian that helps governments decide what measures should be brought in to safeguard the bears, and whether laws that already exist should be changed. In Canada, the law fully protects female bears with baby cubs. But when the cubs are about a year old – or to be precise, measure 154 centimetres from head to tail – they and the mothers can be legally killed. Says Ian:

> We are trying to discover just how soon young cubs can hunt on their own and be able to survive if their mother is killed. If a hunter is allowed to kill just one bear he will choose the mother from among a family group. Her pelt will be worth more because it is bigger and thicker. We must be sure that the cubs she leaves behind will be able to fend for themselves.

Helping to control a partially immobilised bear

In 1978 we recommended that all family groups should be protected and that only lone adult bears should be killed. Recent studies have shown that cubs which stay with their mothers for two and a half years will survive better than those who leave sooner.

Now, with hunting controlled, there's a new threat. The Arctic is being opened up by oil-men, with exploration and digging on a vast scale. Says Ian, 'As humans investigate and remove natural resources from the sea bed, the local ecology may be upset. We want to make sure that polar bears are disturbed as little as possible, and we can provide advice which may help to protect them.' No matter how the engineers try to keep everything running smoothly, there's always the chance of things going wrong – a major blow-out during drilling, or perhaps large amounts of oil being spilt from a tanker at sea.

'If polar bears were to get covered in oil, they would not be able to control their own body temperatures,' says Ian.

Air trapped by the fur acts as insulation, helping to keep the bears warm. This process is very important to mammals living in such a cold climate. An oiled bear would quickly lose its heat and die.

Also, the bears would try to lick the oil off their hair, and they might eat seals which had been covered with oil. All this would harm the bears internally. And if the seals were killed by an oil-spill, or forced away from the area, the polar bears would have no food. The same thing would happen if the seals' food, fish, were destroyed by oil. The younger, thinner bears would suffer most. They don't have thick layers of body fat to protect them and feed them in a crisis.

Ian Stirling's daughter, Lea, with a young polar bear cub. Its mother has been 'shot' with an immobilising dart

With this potential disaster very much in mind, I asked Ian if he felt the people of Canada were aware of the need for conservation, not just of polar bears but of all wildlife.

More and more Canadians are becoming aware, but we are very fond of our home comforts! As a nation, I don't think we take conservation seriously enough – yet.

Television can be an important way of telling people about wildlife and the possible dangers. We have a couple of good programmes in Canada – and a few not so good! I believe such programmes must always be accurate and never sentimental.

I must admit I am worried about the rate at which the industrialised world is using up natural resources. We are wasting enormous amounts of oil and other products which cannot be replaced. I just hope humans learn to be a little less wasteful. The world population is continuing to grow at a frightening rate and richer countries must not just share their wealth with poorer ones, but also the knowledge of how to use it to achieve a higher quality of life.

And what of the polar bear – what are its chances of long-term survival? Says Ian:

I'm optimistic, because of the sort of work we are doing. But you must remember that the polar bear has a very slow breeding rate. At most, the female has only two cubs every three years. If a disaster happened to them, it would take a long time to build up numbers again.

This is one of the reasons why we need the sort of information that I spend my life collecting. We need to plan for the future, and we can only do that if we know from research what will be best for the species.

But I think we are on the right track in Canada as far as polar bears are concerned. My work is fascinating, and I'm delighted that the results are helping polar bears to survive in their natural surroundings.

Allan Thornton

Allan Thornton

Not long ago, the phone rang on my office desk just a few minutes before I was going out 'on air' with that day's edition of *Newsround*. It was someone from the conservation group Greenpeace telling me that their famous flagship, the *Rainbow Warrior*, had been arrested off the coast of Newfoundland in Canada.

The ship's crew had been trying to interfere with the annual hunt of baby seals in the icefloes by covering their beautiful white coats with a green dye that would make them worthless to the killers.

Not just the ship was arrested. Also charged was Allan Thornton, a soft-spoken 31-year-old Canadian who is one of the top men in Greenpeace. He had been out on the ice, marking the seal pups when the Government helicopters swooped down.

The story got on *Newsround*, and in many newspapers all around the world. The *Rainbow Warrior* was taken to the nearest port, two days' sailing away, and a court case followed. Greenpeace and its men on the ice were found guilty and fined – but they had made their point. It had been a typical voyage for the *Rainbow Warrior*.

From his cramped and scruffy office in London, Allan Thornton organises some of the most sensational, most effective crusades ever waged in the cause of wildlife. Seal hunting is one of his big concerns, but his greatest mission is to save the whales.

Alan has spearheaded a number of dramatic, some would say foolhardy, expeditions which have involved sailing in small boats right between the whales and the men who are trying to kill them with harpoons. 'We have a responsibility,' he says, 'to pass the earth on to the next generation in as least as good a state as we received it.'

> What has been happening to the whales is very important, not just because it shows how greedily and cruelly they are hunted, but because it shows how man is hurting nature. For example, two particular kinds of whale are coming ashore and dying on the beaches at the moment, and no-one knows why they are doing it. It may well be that it's caused by

Pilot whales stranded on an Australian beach

something which is being put into the sea by humans; we have to find out what it is.

Whales have literally been cooked alive by acids fed into the sea from factories in Italy. And as far as hunting is concerned, I don't think anyone has the right to destroy something for profit just because they've got the right equipment to do it.

Since ancient times, whales have had a rather special place in the life of the world. In Vietnam, people think of them as 'chivalrous knights' who are sent by the God of the Sea to look after fishermen and sailors in peril. Anyone who finds a dead whale on the beaches has to go into mourning for three months.

Eskimos chase and kill whales, but they hold them in respect. Until the last century fishermen in Iceland believed that 'good' whales drove shoals of herring

111

towards their nets – unless men were fighting each other nearby. Certain kinds of 'good' whale were left alone, and when modern whaling ships began to hunt anything in sight, the fishermen protested, but without success.

There are more than eighty different kinds of whales, and the 'family' also includes dolphins and porpoises. Some of the smaller types have strange names like the Scamper-Down and the Flat-headed Bottle-nosed whales. But the ones that are hunted with harpoons – big metal spears attached to strong cables – are the Great Whales, and there are nine species of these.

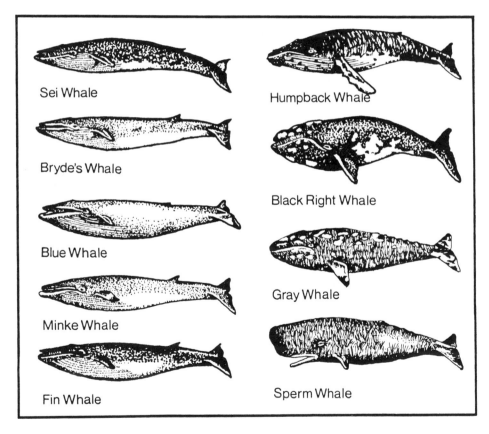

The nine Great Whales

One reason they've been persecuted so much is that almost every part of their huge bodies can be turned into something useful. In Japan, for instance, people eat whalemeat from tins, just like baked beans or sardines! Whalebones are used to make things as different as umbrellas and chessmen. Whale oil has been a vital ingredient in soap, perfumes and crayons, and the tendons were turned into strings for tennis rackets. Nowadays, there are man-made alternatives for all these things, but the hunting still goes on.

So many have been killed that, some years ago, scientists began to wonder whether certain species might be wiped out altogether. A great international argument began about how many whales should be slaughtered in a year. And that was where Greenpeace and Allan Thornton came in. But before I tell you what happened, let's find out a little more about Allan himself.

He was born and brought up in Windsor, in the state of Ontario, Canada, just across the border from America and the huge, industrial city of Detroit. He says he grew up with terrible pollution in the air and water close by, but didn't really understand what was going on until years later.

He remembers walking as a child along the shores of one of the Great Lakes, Lake Erie, and finding them lined with dead fish, killed by chemicals that had been poured into the lake from the factories of Detroit. 'If you drove a car, you had to be extra careful on the days when the wind was blowing ash from one particular factory,' he says. 'The ash contained acid which "ate" away the paint.'

By the time he left Windsor to travel west to Vancouver, he was worried about what was happening to the environment, but hadn't found a way of doing anything about it. Vancouver was a much nicer place to live in; it was on the sea, the air was cleaner, and there were mountains nearby. He took odd jobs as a waiter, a woodmill worker and a porter while trying to write novels and organising college courses for other writers.

As it happened, Vancouver was the base for Greenpeace, a rather loosely-connected group of people who organised protest campaigns about the hunting of whales and seals, and about the dangers of testing nuclear bombs. Greenpeace was founded in 1969 by people who wanted to stop a nuclear bomb from being tested on a distant island in the Pacific Ocean. (At first the group had another name – the Don't Make A Wave Committee.) Instead of just printing leaflets and making speeches, they decided to try and actually prevent the nuclear test themselves, without doing anything violent.

As a result, about twenty people sailed into the test area in small boats, and though the bomb was later exploded future tests were cancelled as a result of the protest. The story made big news, and millions of people heard about their campaign for the first time.

Expeditions like that are both difficult and expensive, but in 1972 the committee's chairman, a remarkable Canadian called David McTaggart, decided to try one again. He and two friends sailed into a zone in the Pacific where the French government was planning to test a nuclear bomb. They managed to delay the test for several weeks; and there was a great hue and cry when news got back that a French ship had rammed McTaggart's little boat. Later, on the day the bomb was due to go off, French sailors boarded the boat and tried to beat up the three men. Photographs of that incident were shown around the world – and McTaggart had got his message home.

Just about the time that Allan Thornton was moving to Vancouver the group, by then called Greenpeace, was using a rather bigger vessel. The idea was to track down a Russian whaling ship and draw attention to the wholesale slaughter of the world's biggest creatures.

They followed the ship for two months, trying to

interfere with its schedule of killing, and also made things difficult for smaller whaling ships in the Pacific. They used exactly the same technique that was first used in those demonstrations against the nuclear tests: getting themselves into a position where their opponents couldn't do their work without harming them.

It was an exciting, dangerous time for the Greenpeace team. When a boat with a harpoon began chasing a whale that had shown itself above the waves, the demonstrators would set out in their small, inflatable boat. They'd try to get between the harpoon gun and the whale, so that anyone firing the harpoon would risk spearing the men in the inflatable. That way, the whale sometimes escaped. I've seen film of this daring action on the high seas, and it looks like a scene from an adventure movie – though the reason for it is, of course, very serious.

Greenpeace's methods of saving wildlife became controversial, and some people criticised them for the headline-catching way they went about things. But their name was getting known, and when one of their ships left Vancouver on a whale-saving voyage, 20,000 people were on the quay to wave goodbye.

By now, Allan was fully involved with the Greenpeace group, helping to back up, on land, everything that was happening at sea. He began selling posters, badges, T-shirts, and bumper stickers. He got together a sales team to raise money and became the top 'badge' salesman himself. When things were going well, he alone brought in £300 a week to the Greenpeace headquarters. The group had taken its new name because green was the colour chosen by many environmental groups around the world, and it wanted to emphasise that its message was a peaceful approach to nature.

With his own limited savings, Allan travelled to Europe to spread the word. He met people who felt the same way – comedian Spike Milligan supported him in public, and ex-Beatle George Harrison gave him a little money to start a Greenpeace base in London. If, at first, Greenpeace had had the reputation of being a bit 'freaky', it was now starting to be taken seriously.

In 1977, Allan had his first taste of what it was like at the 'sharp end' of a Greenpeace campaign. Accompanied by a lawyer, photographers and a film crew, Allan and another Greenpeace worker, Paul, took a helicopter out to the seal hunt off the Newfoundland coast just at the time that the ice floes were beginning to break up. Their aim was to hamper the hunt, which they believed was cruel because of the way the pups were clubbed to death. There was also a threat, they claimed, that Harp seals could become endangered because the pups were dying in such large numbers.

'I remember looking at this piece of ice,' said Allan. 'It was about thirty metres wide and being moved around by huge waves and there were piece of shifting ice all over the place. We were three kilometres away from the hunt itself which was based around a ship.' Allan and Paul set off across this floating, dangerous crazy-paving of ice, and it took them three hours to reach the hunt. Close up, Allan was stunned by what he saw. 'I saw a club come down on a seal pup's head and the noise was horrible. The violence was disgusting.'

Allan and Paul did what they could: they lay on top of the little seals to protect them, and even stood in front of the ship, on an ice floe 'about as big as a room' while the ship pushed it along. Paul scrambled alongside the ship and handcuffed himself to the cable which was being used to haul the bundles of seal skins onto the deck. The hunters got their revenge by pulling the cable up and down, dipping the helpless Paul several times into the icy sea. Allan seized a dinghy and pulled him out, but eventually they had to make peace with the hunters to get Paul onto the ship and warmed up.

What happened on the Newfoundland ice helped convince Greenpeace that they needed their own ocean-

Getting the Rainbow Warrior *ready for sea*

going base. Back in London, they started to look around for a boat they could afford to buy. Eventually, Denise Bell and Susie Newborn (two other members of Greenpeace) found a ship that had once been used for scientific expeditions, and before they'd raised anything like the cash they needed, they'd had their bid accepted. They were able to put down a 10% deposit on the price of £45,000 and were given two months to find the rest. Finally, they haggled the price down by £13,000!

The ship was handed over in January 1978 – and they wanted to set out to the North Atlantic whaling grounds five months later. 'The boat,' says Allan, 'was the biggest pile of junk you could imagine. To make things worse, none of us knew a thing about boats. At the beginning, we even found it hard to find the light switches!' Allan and an Australian colleague moved in to live on the boat and they sent out an appeal for help in getting it ready for sea. Every Saturday, at least twenty-five volunteers were down at the West India docks in London, scraping old coats of paint off the hull. People with useful skills gave their time free: welders, electricians, carpenters and engineers. By the beginning of May, what had been a rusting hulk once called the *Sir William Hardy* had been transformed into Greenpeace's flagship the *Rainbow Warrior*.

At that time, there was special concern about one of the species of Great Whales called the Fin Whale. Allan suggested that *Rainbow Warrior* should tackle the whaling fleets based in Iceland which hunted the Fin whale. The campaign was carefully timed – that year's meeting of the International Whaling Commission was due to hear a proposal that all whaling should stop for at least ten years. The boat and its crew of twenty made its way slowly – testing its seaworthiness as it went – to the whaling area via Calais, Rotterdam, Hamburg and the Orkneys. Eventually they arrived in the south of Iceland, and the hunt for the hunters was on.

It was not easy. The whaling boats moved at 15 knots and *Rainbow Warrior*'s top speed was only 10 knots. The crew spent two exhausting weeks trying to get close enough to stop a hunting boat which had spotted its prey. They failed and, downhearted, they sailed into the

A volunteer helps to paint the Rainbow Warrior

Icelandic capital, Reyjavik, and held a public debate about the whaling controversy. Then they set out again.

Within a day, they spotted a whaler that was getting into position to harpoon some whales playing near the surface. In fact, the *Rainbow Warrior* was six kilometres from the action, so two small inflatable boats were launched. Allan remembers spending the whole bumpy journey holding onto the engine's petrol tank with his foot, in case it fell off.

The next few minutes were 'the most stunning experience of my whole life.' As they came closer to the whaler they could see that it had caught one whale. These kinds of whalers try to catch three whales in a 30-hour period, and then head back to port so that the meat stays fresh. The Greenpeace men knew that if they could get in the

The Rainbow Warrior *sets out on one of its first campaigns (1978)*

way for long enough, the boat would run out of time and have to return to port without its last two whales.

So they tried to keep the inflatables in front of the harpoon, but the hunting boat turned out to be very manoeuvrable and hard to keep up with. Occasionally, whales would break the surface nearby, and the dinghies, tossing about among the huge waves, managed to get between the whales and the whaling boats.

The crewman behind the harpoon, who was mounted on a special platform in the bows, seemed helpless – he wasn't sure what to do. Then Allan saw the boat's captain run down the catwalk and seize the harpoon himself. Two whales came up for air not far away, and Allan's boat was directly between the harpoon and one of them. 'I thought he was going to shoot. We put the inflatable as close to the whales as we possible could without running over them. He kept the harpoon aimed and I had the feeling I was going to die in a few seconds.'

Finally, the frustrated captain put the safety catch back on the harpoon and gave up. But he kept looking out for whales for five hours while the inflatable trailed him around in case he should try again. The little boats eventually returned to the *Rainbow Warrior* and their tired but happy crews were just eating hot soup and sandwiches when somebody yelled 'He's hunting again!' They had to clamber back and start all over again. But

A Grey seal cub from the Orkneys

the hunting boat finally went back to port with only one whale; two whales had been saved.

That was just the start of the *Rainbow Warrior*'s adventures. The trip ended with some debts to pay off and a special fund-raising campaign was mounted. But she was soon off again: to the Orkneys to interrupt a seal hunt; trying to blockade a Norwegian port so that sealing boats couldn't put to sea; and being 'arrested' by Spanish gunboats after stopping some Spanish whalers from catching anything for three days running. The *Rainbow Warrior* also launched her little boats against ships dropping canisters of radioactive nuclear waste into the sea hundreds of kilometres off the French coast. Once, a 250 kg canister smashed into one of the dinghies as it was being dumped. Greenpeace and other environmental groups say that there are risks that containers will leak and the dangerous waste will get into the sea; governments reply that the dumping is perfectly safe. Greenpeace has recently bought a second boat unofficially called Warrior II.

With its actions at sea, and its campaigns on land, Greenpeace was helping to create a new awareness about some of the threats that face our natural world. A public inquiry into whaling was held in Australia. The British government changed its position to support the call for a ban on whaling altogether. More research was ordered into the complicated business of exactly how many whales of each kind there are, how they live and how many should be allowed to be killed. The Dutch government, followed by the French, supported the move to suspend whaling. Meanwhile, Allan was in charge of Greenpeace's London office, presiding over a growing variety of campaigns on environmental issues: oil pollution, chemical waste disposal, pesticide and nuclear power.

Of the whale campaign, Allan says:

I'm encouraged by the gains we have made. We've battled for ten years and there's been a

Using inflatable boats, members of Greenpeace position themselves between the Spanish whalers and the whales so that the Spanish can't shoot (1980)

substantial improvement which there wouldn't have been otherwise. The quota of 50,000 whales caught each year has been brought down to 13,500, and that's not bad. The threat of hunting is receding all the time. Soon I think the International Whaling Commission will halt whaling completely – at least for a time. But there are always other threats to life in the sea; man's influence is almost always destructive in some way.

Allan is a vegetarian and thinks that the unnecessary killing of any animal is wrong, so naturally he backs the argument that whales are killed in a needlessly cruel fashion. 'I've seen a whale harpooned and it's not a pretty sight. It can take a Minke whale an hour to die. Its pain must be communicated to other whales because we know

now that whales "talk" to each other. The more we learn about them, the more we realise what we don't know.'

So much killing isn't necessary. It doesn't serve an essential purpose and it brutalises the people who carry it out. That's why whales are not just important for themselves – they symbolise how we behave towards nature.

Acknowledgments

The Publishers would like to thank the following people and organisations for providing photographs.

Associated Press *52,111*   Australian Information Service, London *35,37,39,40,41,43,45*   Daily Telegraph *50,57,60* Chris Fairclough *8,13,14,27*   Greenpeace *109,117,119,120,121, 123*   Kes Hillman *67,69,70,72,78*   Alan Howard *17* Peter Jackson *63,75*   Royal Society for the Protection of Birds *79,80,83,86,88,90*   Vincent Serventy *29,32*   Ian Stirling *93,94,95,97,99,100,101,102,103,105,107*   P M Snyder *66* Thames Television *54,55*   Philip Wayre *20,22,25*

Index

Queensland *38*

Rainbow Warrior *110,118, 119,121,122*
rat kangaroo *36*
red kangaroo *36*
Reyjavik *119*
rhino *63,64,65,67,68,71,73,76*
Rhino Group *67,68*
Robinson (Peter) *11, 79–92*
rock wallaby *36*
Rotterdam *118*
Royal Society for the Protection of Birds (RSPB) *80,81,82,83*

Sandy (Bedfordshire) *81*
Saudi Arabia *74*
Scamper-Down whale *112*
Scotland *83,84*
scrub-bird *42,43,45,47*
seal *95,96,100,103,106,110*
sea-urchin 60
Serventy (Vincent) *11, 29–48*
sheep *34,35,38*
Sheffield *91*
songbird *89*
Southern White rhino *70*
South Africa *76*
South America *53*
South Korea *73*
Soviet Union *103*
Stirling (Ian) *11, 93–108*
Sudan *69,76*
Sumatran rhino *73*
Sydney *42*

Taiwan *73*
Tanzania *68,71*
Tasmania *38*
Thornton (Allan) *11, 109–123*
Torrey Canyon *52*
tree kangaroo *38*

Uganda *68,69*
United States *103*

Vancouver *113,114,115*
Venice *53*
Vietnam *111*

wallaby *36*
'walkabout' *32*
wasp *47*
Wayre (Philip) *10,11, 13–28*
whale *110,119,120,121,122, 123*
White rhino *69*
Wildlife and Countryside Bill (1981) *58,92*
Windsor (Ontario) *113*
wolf *17*
wolverines *17*
wombat *34*
World Wildlife Fund *27,46,71, 75*

Young Ornithologists Club *10*

Zambia *71,72*